BREAKING FREE

A SAGA OF SELF-DISCOVERY BY
A GAY SECRET SERVICE AGENT

A Memoir by Cory Allen

Copyright © 2023 Cory Allen
Printed in the United States of America
Breaking Free: A Saga of Self-Discovery by a Gay Secret Service Agent / Allen-
1st Edition

ISBN: 978-1-953610-62-1

        1. Memoir> LGBTQ+
        2. LGBTQ+ Biographies
        3. Personal Transformation
        4. United States Secret Service> Books
        5. LGBTQ+ Demographic Studies

NFB
<<<>>>
NFB Publishing/Amelia Press
119 Dorchester Road
Buffalo, New York 14213

For more information visit
Nfbpublishing.com

Certain people and events in this memoir have been altered to protect the identities of those involved and to respect government agencies. The opinions expressed are solely those of the author. In no way do they represent any government group, including the U.S. Air Force, Virginia Air National Guard, Hanover County Sheriff's Office, U.S. Department of Homeland Security, or the United States Secret Service.

Author's Note:

What began as a note on my phone as a fleeting idea and a way to organize my thoughts, has come to life. It's hard to believe. Thank you to my fiancé Johnny for your love and patience, my amazing family, friends (David and Tonny, especially), my Secret Service family who got me through so much, Michelle and Barack Obama, and my first boyfriend. I wouldn't be who I am today without our relationship.

A special shout-out to my editor Jay Blotcher. I hope to have the honor to work with you again in the future.

CHAPTER ONE

May 2020

DAY SIXTY OF THE shelter-in-place order. The time is flying by, though the days blend together more than they normally would. I have been fortunate enough to be able to work from home during the COVID-19 pandemic. Therefore, I have not been too inconvenienced despite a lack of social activity or travel. It took a week or two for me to mentally adjust to the new reality, develop a routine, figure out how to instill self-care (mental and physical), and determine what working from home would look like.

Without a normal schedule, routine to adhere to, and a new-found abundance of time indoors, it was a logical time to sit at my desk and begin the process of writing about everything circling in my mind; where I'd been, what I'd done, how I ended up in a studio apartment three thousand miles from my family.

After a short stint in Fresno, I moved to San Francisco last fall, choosing a new studio apartment on Market Street. I wanted the benefit of living in the city, plus all of its conveniences: no need to own a car, walkability to Castro, and numerous parks to walk Simba, my Shetland Sheepdog.

I had just marked the one-year anniversary of leaving the U.S.

Secret Service in Washington, D.C., leaving my family, my friends, and everything I knew in search of a better and more balanced life. It's taken some time for my mind to catch up with my body and mentally process everything that transpired over the last few years, after living life at a chaotic pace for so long. Time escapes us at a tempo few of us ever realize. As I look back, I can definitely say it's been a whirlwind, with few opportunities to reflect upon significant life events. The years have flown by since I was in the military, which happened before becoming a police officer. Then I was a Secret Service agent, requiring multiple moves around the country, and coming to terms with who I really was. This involved a divorce, leaving a job behind that consumed my identity near the peak of my career, and the periodic relationships I've had since my divorce.

I'm incredibly fortunate to be able to take a moment to reflect upon my past while plotting out my future, hoping to achieve even greater things.

I am originally from Indiana, PA, a small town in western Pennsylvania in the heart of coal and Steeler country. The entire extended family, including grandparents and cousins, lived in that area. My grandfather Robert Henry was a man who stood six feet tall with a slender yet muscular frame. He had adopted my mother from a young age and adopted several other children, all whom he raised on the farm he and my grandma LaRue built and owned. My family lived about a mile away from the farm, over the hill and cow pasture. That was my childhood home.

My father Harry was a carpenter and worked for the construction company that my paternal grandfather had started in the 1940s. Dad built the house. I fondly remember the simple three-bedroom house I shared with my two older brothers Rich and Rob (twins that are two years my elder). I was born in late 1979. Our home sat on forty acres of woods and fields. We lived there until late 1987.

My memories in that home involve playing endlessly with my brothers outdoors, and sometimes being locked out of the house to give mom her reprieve. We would walk the woods, fields, and pastures to get to our grandparents' house, or play with nearby cousins. I recall exploring the creeks and making boats out of fallen trees and sticks. Given that we didn't have a lot of money nor a toy store nearby, we made do with whatever nature gave us. We spent long days running through skunk cabbage, building forts, and running around freely while bears roamed the area. How we never got injured or drowned is beyond me, given the lack of supervision.

My maternal grandfather was larger than life. Robert Franklin Henry was lovingly known as "Pap." He was the patriarch of our family, as well as my mentor, role model, and hero. Pap was a member of the Greatest Generation, signing up to serve in World War II at the age of 29. He had to visit several different recruiting stations since he was too old. Finally, he was enlisted in the United States Army Air Corps (the Air Force didn't exist until 1947). Pap was a member of the 96th Bomb Group, 337th Bomb Squadron in the European theatre. He was a tail gunner in a B-17 Flying Fortress named Wabbit-Twacks III, tail number 42-30040.

Unlike many war vets, Pap was happy to talk about his war days and he'd go on for hours. He was shot down on October 14, 1943, while returning from a mission in Schweinfurt, Germany. He was secreted by the French underground for seven months. Pap was ultimately captured by the Gestapo along the Spanish border and held as a prisoner of war. He was lucky that he was captured in the European theatre, he told us, as those captured in the Pacific theatre were either tortured or murdered. Pap was forced to walk eight hundred miles before being liberated by the British 2nd Army on May 2, 1945.

Upon returning home to Indiana County, Pap took up life as a farmer, rural mail courier, and a family man. He and Grandma were unable to have biological children and they began adopting four children in the early 1950's and adopted Mom in 1959.

Mom and Dad married in 1976 and my brothers were born in 1977. Dad is over six feet tall with a muscular frame and dark hair, looking a lot like rock singer Bob Seger except he had a belly as long as I can remember. I certainly got my height from him, at six feet two inches but no belly since I only weigh one-hundred and seventy pounds and straight brown hair. During the day, Dad was a contractor building homes. At night, he could be found working on cars. Dad was a skilled carpenter and, to this day, can create astonishing things with his hands, from exquisite staircases to backyard gazebos. Dad also enjoyed racing cars and had a Camaro Z28 that was used for drag racing. Mom was a five-foot, four-inch woman with piercing blue eyes and brown hair. She was in nursing school in the late-1970s and an EMT, a profession she still has today. The four of them lived in a trailer on my grandparents' farm while our home was being built. I unexpectedly came along in October 1979. Luckily, the home was complete. I don't remember a lot from those first few years, but I recall one significant incident. One evening in 1982, when I was only two, there was a dispute between Mom and Dad. It involved ample yelling, Mom sobbing, and Dad punching through a door before stomping out of the house. I remember holding onto her leg and looking up at her after Dad left. I don't have many memories of my father being around after that. I was later told Dad was selfish back then and was part of the problem why he and mom split up but the entirety of the story remains a mystery to me.

Sometime after that, Mom introduced us to Bob. Bob was a tall, very slender guy, who had an awkward laugh but an uncanny ability to make everyone else laugh along with him. He never seemed to take himself seriously and I never saw him lose his temper or treat anyone in the house poorly. He genuinely seemed to love making Mom and us happy. Bob turned out to be an amazing stand-in father. He loved us as his own. Bob treated Mom well and played with us. He'd give us rides on this motorcycle scooter thing. Winters in western Pennsylvania can dump a lot of snow and I remember one-year Bob helped us build igloos in the yard. They were large enough that we could play in them. Bob had become the best stepfather. I'd grown to love his awkward laugh, his sense of humor, and how he made Mom smile. It was like having a grown child in the house, except I never got in fights with this one, unlike my siblings.

It was Christmas season 1985, when I was six years old. My brothers were in school and Mom was asleep after her night shift. Since I only had kindergarten every other day, Bob took me shopping for presents. As we shopped, Bob explicitly told me not to tell Mom what we were doing. I promised. But when we got home, Mom asked what where we had been. I blurted out proudly that we had gone Christmas shopping to buy her a can opener. I still can't lie to save my life.

I still don't know why things didn't work out between Mom and Bob. I just know that one day in 1985 he was gone. I wasn't given an explanation, and, in our adulthood, my brothers and I have never spoken of it.

In 1985, Mom met Dan. Dan was another tall and dark-haired man, around six feet with jet black hair. Dan was into stock car racing. One of the first things I noticed was he only had four fingers on one of his hands. He'd lost the finger in a racing accident prior to meeting Mom. Whenever he'd hold my hand, I was always cognizant of that missing digit. Dan was another guy who had a great sense of humor and was fun to be around. Dan's parents were very loving people who lived on a hill that overlooked a creek. We visited often. Their home was known for an endless supply of sweets and soft drinks. Mom and Dan married in April of 1986, and all the males in the wedding party wore baby blue suits. Dan was welcomed into the clan, and he loved the three of us as his own. He was an amazing stepfather. (He still is, if you ignore his fabricated Facebook postings and his far-right-wing conspiracies.)

Mom and Dan were good parents, but things got a little odd sometimes. Let's say they had a strange sense of humor. And I am still feeling the effects of it. For some odd reason, Mom and Dan would force us to sit in front of the TV and watch horror movies when I was about eight and my brothers were about ten. We'd watch stuff like *Friday the 13th* and *Child's Play*, so that we got to know the insane killers Jason and Chuckie.

At some point during the movies, Mom and Dan would quietly sneak out of the house without us knowing. Keep in mind that we lived in the middle of nowhere. Then they would pound on the living room windows and door to scare the hell out of us. I would jump, yelping in terror while Mom and Dan laughed heartily.

One evening following a horror show, we were getting ready for bed. I walked into my bedroom to put clothes in the hamper in the closet. As I pulled at the doorknob, the closet door suddenly swung open. Out jumped a giant ape. It scared me so much that I leapt backward, hit the bed, flipped over, and landed against the wall. This was another sick joke hatched between Mom and Dan.

Mom was prone to spontaneous and impulsive car buying. Dan was encouraging her. Our family cars were unconventional, as a result. We had a white GMC truck (we rode in the back) and a 1981 Camaro Z28, neither vehicle legally holding five persons. When we rode around town in the back seat of the Camaro, I recall seeing the 8-track player sticking out from the console. Mom had an abundance of 8-track tapes. This was the first instance where music would weave itself through my life. Moms go to tapes were Survivor, Air Supply, 38 Special, and Foreigner, with the latter two making enough impressions upon me to memorize and sing along with the songs. There was something about the melodic beats and lyrics that permeated my young brain and enabled me to memorize them easily, as well as the order of the songs on the tapes.

One night in March 1987 when I was almost eight, I recall some commotion in the house and frantic calls being made to my grandparents. I went into the bathroom and saw blood but wasn't sure what had occurred. Turns out, Mom had gone into labor and my sister Stacie was born a short time later in the hospital. I was promptly moved into the bedroom with my older brothers and my room became the nursery. To me, this wasn't ideal, because my older brothers were always a team. So, I spent a lot of time interacting with my new sister.

In October of that year, we moved to Mechanicsville, Virginia, a suburb of Richmond, since Dan had found a job working at a concrete plant. Until then, Dan had been traveling to the Richmond area seeking work and spending many nights sleeping in his truck. Once we moved, it would be easier for Mom to get a job as a nurse. Richmond had many more options than Western Pennsylvania, given its terrible economy since they closed the coal mines.

I was saddened by the move, mostly because we would be moving away from our grandparents. That meant no more sleepovers at the farm, no more sleeping out under the stars, or falling down hay chutes in the barn. I loved spending time on the farm. Pap would always include us in tasks around the farm, allowing us to ride on the tractors, steering them, or ride on the hay wagons. I was too young to actually help out, but he never shied away from including us. I jumped at every opportunity to help mow the grass and drive the riding lawnmower, the closest thing at my age to driving a car. He always made me feel special and loved.

Pap was the softie when it came to the grandchildren and often caved in to our demands. He often took me to Norma Jean's restaurant for fried shrimp or ice cream. Before bed, he would allow me to have a "midnight snack," which was usually a bowl of Count Chocula or Boo Berry cereal. All I ever wanted was Pap's approval and to be a fraction of the man he was. His words carried weight like no other.

My grandparents were known for having tons of spare change and money around the house. One day, my eldest brother convinced us that it was a good idea to take some the money for ourselves. We got caught. Pap sat me down, looked me in the eye and said, "I'm disappointed in you." It was crushing to me and made me cry. There was no spanking or other punishment, just the weight of his words and they were effective. I'll forever be grateful to have had this amazing man in my life as my moral compass. He shaped me in ways he may have never known.

I remember the first day I saw our new home. We pulled into Cold Harbor Gardens, the apartment community in Mechanicsville, and I was in awe at the size of it. I was confused as it was the first time I'd seen an apartment complex. We had to all transfer schools since the school year was already underway and I ended up having Ms. Young as my second-grade teacher. Ms. Young was Miss Virginia at some point in her life. She was tall and pretty with curly red hair and she reminded me of Reba McEntire. The most prominent memory from that year was where I attempted to forge my Mom's signature on a note that had been sent home. As a result, I was sent to Mom and Dan's bedroom and told to stand at the waterbed and receive my spanking with a wooden paddle. I never forged a note again.

In 1987, my paternal grandparents Henry and Margaret sent us gifts in the mail for Christmas. The gifts had been the first communication from my father's side of the family in about five years. It was my grandmother's idea to track us down. We three boys partially opened the gifts to see what they were, and then discreetly re-taped them shut. I was excited to hear from them, have gifts from them, and begin making visits to see them again. They always had great gifts, rock-hard, sugar-free candy in the glove box, drives to go for ice cream, a fun basement to play in, and we'd sit on the front porch people-watching as the sun set over the Northern Cambria valley. I doubt I was treated any differently than my siblings, but I viewed myself as the favorite grandchild to Grandma.

That Christmas day, Mom received a phone call. Her mother, LaRue Jean Henry, had passed on. I was eight at the time. All I remember is lots of crying and then a quick exodus to Pennsylvania. Grandma had been suffering from diabetes and given the shortcoming of medical technology, died at only 68 years old. Mom must have felt terrible not being there earlier, having moved the family a couple of months previously.

A funeral through the eyes of an eight-year-old is bizarre. It's almost like it's in third person. Being ushered around from unknown person to unknown person to meet them and have them fuss over you. People are distraught, crying, hugging, while others are telling stories and laughing. I was wildly confused and not knowing how to act.

I recall seeing my grandmother in the coffin, looking fairly like what I remember, but still not knowing exactly what was going on. I wasn't old enough to process the finality of death or sure how the grieving process works. Shortly after Grandma's passing, my grandfather moved into our old home. It felt odd at first, to see him in our old home without grandma but he quickly settled into a routine and we ensured to go home often to spend time with him, even if it was to watch The Price is Right and have lunch at noon. My uncle moved into the farm that my grandfather and Grandma had established. My grandfather moving into my early childhood home would cement that house as "home" for me, the one constant in my periodically disrupted life.

A side effect of the move to Virginia was the six-hour drive we'd endure anytime we would want to visit family in Pennsylvania. To me, the miles seemed to go on forever, and I was usually complaining about stops for a bathroom or to get out of the car for a break. I'd stare out of the window and watch the white lines pass by, looking at other cars and wondering where everyone else was headed—oftentimes being scolded to stop staring at people. Mom always had music on in the car and I found myself singing along to a lot of the country songs that were on the radio. Singing provided an escape from boredom as the miles upon miles passed by. I would try my best to mimic George Strait, Restless Heart, John Anderson, or Shenandoah songs. It just sprang from me. It felt good. Pretty soon I was thinking how cool it would feel to be able to sing and do that as a job.

CHAPTER TWO

.

GROWING UP IN MECHANICSVILLE, VIRGINIA, was generally fine, as it seemed easy to meet new people since the community had lots of similar families in it. The apartments, known as Cold Harbor Gardens at the time, seemed to be full of kids to play with, whereas life in Pennsylvania had mostly been me and my brothers on our own – and occasional time with cousins. There were playgrounds and a pool that was the hub of activity in the summertime. By this point in 1988, I was almost nine and Mom had become a nurse. She was working midnight shifts at Richmond Memorial Hospital. The graveyard shifts usually paid a little more and raising four children wasn't cheap, even in the 1980s. Dan continued working at the concrete plant but due to the abundance of new social activities to engage in, I didn't pay a lot of attention to what was going on at home.

Between 1988 and 1989, things began to go south between Mom and Dan. I remember tending to my sister some nights when Mom was at work because Dan just wasn't around. On one occasion, my brothers and I went outside to play with our friends. The front door got locked while our sister Stacie was inside of it. I was terrified and the apartment management had to be called to get the door unlocked. I felt like I'd let Mom down. Even at this young age, I felt like I was the more responsible child of the three brothers and should have known better.

One afternoon, new bunk beds were being set for my brothers. In one bedroom, mattresses had been stacked against the window. I was outside, playing with neighbors. One of my brothers was on top of the mattresses with my sister Stacie at the window, behind the screen. Somehow Stacie fell out of the second-floor window. As she fell, her head struck the brick ledge of the first-floor window before she landed in the bushes. I rushed over, picked her up from the bush, and ran up the stairs and into our apartment. There was a lot of blood, but Mom was home, and an ambulance took Stacie to the hospital. Thankfully, there were no long-term effects, and my sister made a full recovery.

Living in an apartment complex allows you to meet all kinds of people and have access to very different things. One day, when I was nine, I discovered a back massager and Playgirl magazines underneath of Mom's bed in our apartment. Another day, I found a Hustler magazine in the bushes of our apartment building. After looking through the porn, I would hide them again in the massive hedges, repeatedly for a few weeks. I was turned on by these images but in my immature mind, I didn't have the ability to think any deeper about it. But I also felt ashamed about what I was doing. On top of all that, I also wanted to keep it as my secret, uncertain how my brothers would react. My private sex education continued until the groundskeepers found the magazines and trashed them. I was saddened that my secret porno stash mag was now gone, and I no longer had a reason to visit the bushes.

Not long after my sister's accident, we moved into a ground-floor apartment in the same complex. During the move, this guy appeared out of nowhere in his orange Chevy pickup to help us move. This would be my first introduction to a massive man who went by the name Hollywood. He was larger than life to me—not only tall, but muscular. Hollywood was over six feet tall and weighed about two hundred and fifty pounds. He had a curly mullet, a light brown beard, a great smile, and an outgoing personality. He looked remarkably similar to the country singer Travis Tritt. Before I realized it, Hollywood was living with us in the new apartment, complete with a wooden clock on the wall that had three women in bikinis in the back of a pickup truck and the words "Haulin Ass" on it. He treated us kids well. He was playful with us and he was especially fond of Stacie, since he didn't have any children of his own. He knew how to cook and was often found in the kitchen preparing meals from deer or turkey he'd hunted. It was nice to have him around and I enjoyed his cooking, mainly his venison jerky and country biscuits but never his nasty "dressing" he made, which was his substitute for stuffing.

My brothers, Rich and Rob, were getting to the age that they were always outside playing with friends and I was the one who looked after my sister, so I felt we were affected far greater by Hollywood than they were. I discovered that Hollywood was an avid marijuana user. I found small plants growing in the apartment and observed him rolling joints and smoking. I had no idea what these plants were and one day when I found one in the closet, I took a giant whiff of the leaf. It was nauseating but I was intrigued to the point that one day I rolled up oregano in a paper towel and tried to smoke it. Thankfully, I didn't burn the apartment down. I also found Marlboro menthol cigarettes in the apartment and would sit on the back steps smoking, at the ripe old age of ten. I coughed at first, but it seemed like the hip thing to do at the time. My surrogate father would take me on rides in his truck as he smoked his marijuana. Hollywood also drank a lot of Budweiser; the empty cans always seemed to be floorboard of the truck. We'd also collect the cans from the house and cash them in at the recycling center.

Hollywood was also an avid outdoorsman, taking me along on hunting trips on weekends or school holidays. Truth be told, I was miserable hunting. It was usually cold, wet, and early in the morning. But I went along so I wouldn't disappoint him. I did enjoy shooting the .22 rifle at cans, bottles, and in the general direction of squirrels. But I failed at bagging any animals. On one hunting trip, Hollywood let me to drink a few cans of Budweiser, giving me my first drunken experience at the age of 11. I drank four cans of beer and my vision had grown blurry before I was cut off.

Little did we know, hiding beneath Hollywood's country boy exterior there was a giant, fucked-up evil side.

His first episode of domestic violence occurred within a couple of months of moving in with us. Boy, was it heated. I was eleven and my sister was three. I recall Hollywood chasing Mom down the hall and into the back bedroom of our apartment. Once the door slammed shut, all I could hear was Mom's muffled screaming for help, mostly calling my name since my brothers weren't home. I sensed her shrill and terrifying screams were due to being beaten. I didn't want to leave my sister alone, but Mom was screaming my name for help and I panicked; I jumped out of the window and ran to a neighbor's house to call 911. The neighbors were puzzled but they grabbed the phone and called 911 for me. I ran back to the apartment window to comfort Stacie until the police arrived and calmed the situation.

Remembering this incident thirty years later revives emotions that were scarred permanently into my brain. The horror still grips me.

Back in the early 1990s, domestic violence laws were virtually non-existent, and the ones that did exist had no teeth to them. The cops would show up to our apartment after I called, but do very little. Mostly they would calm the dispute, separate the parties, and that was about it. Mom would wear glasses to cover her blackened eyes from Hollywood. I can't fathom the pain and suffering she carried for so long. The neighbors in the complex knew what was going on, but nobody ever offered to help, even when it spilled over into the apartment corridor. I'm certain my grandfather, Pap, knew what was going on. He had met Hollywood and shared some reservations about him but his daughter was several hundred miles away and there wasn't much he could do at the time.

Hollywood and Mom established a pattern that included love, then sudden domestic violence, then the cool-down phase, and a return to the honeymoon period. Then rinse and repeat—for ten long years. I always stayed close to home because of this. I wanted to be there for Stacie and Mom just in case things got heated, especially on Sundays when these were more prone to happen.

Around that same time, our family reestablished contact with my estranged father Harry. After some back and forth with my paternal grandparents, acting as the liaison, we began visiting him again. Grandma and my aunt were the driving forces behind the reunion, desiring to know where we were and how things were going. Mom would meet Dad or my grandparents in Winchester, Virginia, which was the halfway point between our homes, and we'd spend time with our father and grandparents. Dad lived with my grandparents at that time, so it was a huge win to go visit. We got the joys of seeing Dad and being spoiled by Grandma at the same time; what more could a kid ask for! Our cousins lived up the street, so we'd get to play with them when we visited. I loved coming down in the mornings to find a bowl set out for cereal, a small glass of room temperature orange juice, and an endless supply of store-bought Duplex cookies or Grandma's home baked chocolate chip cookies in the brown cookie jar. Being the youngest, I was able to form a closer bond with my father than my siblings at the time, or so I thought anyway. Dad would tape Alf, the TV show, and then watch it with us in the living room and he would hang out with his friends at the Kwik-fill gas station in town and take me along with him. I loved going to the drag racing strip with him and helping in any way I could. At one point I was given the option to move to Pennsylvania with my father. But when it came down to it, I couldn't do it. I wanted to be closer to my father, grandparents, and aunt, but I couldn't imagine growing up away from Mom and my siblings.

Through the years, Mom has confessed some of the prominent domestic violence incidents she suffered at the hands of Hollywood. In one of them, she left for her midnight shift in her Camaro Z28 IROC-Z (not a slow car in it's heyday) and Hollywood snapped and chased her in his Chevy short bed like a madman through Richmond. On another occasion, as they were in their bedroom, he held a gun to her head. At that moment, she swore that she was going to die. But Hollywood suddenly turned the gun on himself and pulled the trigger. Unfortunately, it didn't fire. That sounds awful to say, but it would've saved us years of further abuse. Our family suffered a decade of Hollywood's tirades, tantrums and terrorism—in addition to Mom's periodic beatings. This went on from the time I was nine until I was nineteen. There were incidents involving Hollywood and my brothers, but I was shielded from them and Hollywood usually isn't a topic of conversation when we are all together. Stacie witnessed the most and though she was the youngest, we did the best we could to protect her.

During that decade, we moved multiple times, always staying in the Mechanicsville area. Each time, I'd hope and pray that we'd escape him, but Hollywood always moved with us.

The final straw happened when I was eighteen. It was in the fall of 1997, a typical Sunday when NASCAR was on TV. Hollywood would always drink a ton of beer. If his driver didn't win, it was the first warning sign of danger. That afternoon, Hollywood got verbally abusive with Mom after his driver lost. Fully expecting the worst as the shouting escalated, I called 911. By the time Hanover County Sheriff's Office arrived, the two had calmed down. The cops left and Mom went into work. But after she left, Hollywood's anger turned on me, since I had made the call.

As I nervously sat eating my dinner, a bowl of cereal, Hollywood walked into the kitchen wearing his trademark blue sweatpants and curly mullet, visibly pissed off, and asked if I felt like a badass for calling 911. He grabbed my dinner dish and slammed it against the wall immediately behind me. Then he pinned me against the opposite wall. At eighteen, I was six-foot-two, inches tall, but I was still rail-thin. Hollywood was an inch taller but weighed one hundred pounds more. He announced that since I was now legally an adult, he could legally beat my ass. He didn't strike me, since Stacie was standing in the hallway holding her favorite plush baby doll observing this. But the rage in his eyes told me he had every intention of doing so had she not been there.

Within minutes, Mom came through the front door. She had forgotten something at the house and had returned to retrieve it. Looking at Hollywood and I, she immediately knew something had happened between us. A few months after that episode, Mom finally ended things with Hollywood. She told me that while he could abuse her, she'd never let him mess with one of her children.

I can't fathom how these years of witnessing domestic abuse and uprooting of her life affected Stacie at such a vulnerable age, but she turned out to be an amazing woman—so thankfully, not too much, at least not anything visible. Stacie's father, Dan, had remained in the picture and played an important role through those turbulent years. Often throughout the Hollywood years, I would go with Stacie to spend time with him and escape whatever crisis was going on at home. Dan always treated me like a son. He would take us go-cart racing, out to restaurants, cookouts. He never dropped the ball when it came to parenting Stacie.

Though I had to grow up years before I had preferred, I learned a lot through that decade. I'm forever thankful for the bonds I have with my sister and mother; we are very close and text each other often. We are there to support each other anytime, to talk freely about whatever is going on in our lives. Without Hollywood, ironically, I'm not sure we'd be as close as we are.

Without the negative influence of Hollywood, I may not have

ended up in law enforcement. Due to the frequent interactions with the sheriff's office, I grew to admire what they did, and I realized that I wanted to make a difference for victims like they did for us. It was a primary reason why I entered the career field and that very agency a few years later. So, I can thank Hollywood for an amazing career. He taught me the warning signs and cycle of domestic violence – and especially what *not* to do to women. Jesus Christ, did he mess with our minds and emotions! I'll take a hard pass on reliving that one again.

CHAPTER THREE

I WAS FORTUNATE ENOUGH to end up with a few good friends during adolescence. The first real friend I had was Karl. Karl and his family moved into the apartment in Cold Harbor Gardens that we had first lived in when we moved to Virginia in 1987. I was 10 when Karl and I met. Karl had just moved from Texas and didn't know anyone, so we became fast friends. Karl was two years younger than I was, shorter than I was, with brown eyes and brown hair and looked like the country singer Clint Black. Karl was the quiet type. Karl had an older sister that was my brothers' age and they fawned over her constantly. I could appreciate that she was a pretty girl, but I did not have those same emotional desires that my brothers exhibited.

Karl was my first boy crush. It wasn't until I hit puberty that I realized I was attracted to him and other boys. Karl would be the object of my desires during my teenage years. Though I'd felt confused prior to this realization, I was happy to have a place to channel the urges and desires. I admired his dark brown hair, brown eyes, and body. As puberty progressed, I hoped and hoped that he was just as curious as I was.

During the summer between my sophomore and junior year, we moved into a house that Mom had purchased in Mechanicsville. I had my own room, and it had a king-sized waterbed. The bed was so large that it took up most of the space, but I was happy to finally have my own bedroom. Whenever Karl would stay over on weekends, which was frequent, we slept in the same bed since it was so large, and I would lay awake at night or wake up with a raging teenage erection. He always slept quietly and there was no opportunity to touch each other even accidentally, much to my dismay. I was too scared to make the first move and risk our friendship. I recall the hours I stayed awake, having these homosexual thoughts. I recall the agony of keeping it all hidden from everyone, including my best friend. I could only imagine that I was the only one with these desires.

Our high school was named Lee-Davis, after the Confederate Army heroes. We had a "redneck" row, where all of the pickup trucks parked in the lot, with rebel flags in the backs. All of my friends were straight and they only knew me as straight as well, so I had to suppress any desires and ensure the secret would never get out, for fear of the fallout and potential bullying. All I could do was lust after the boys I thought were cute and look for cues, like eye contact, from them, though they never arrived. I wasn't aware of any gay students in the population and had no resources at my disposal, pre-Internet, to find likeminded students. I never made my same-sex desires known, as Hanover County was deeply conservative, and I was terrified of acting on my desires.

I got my first job two weeks after I turned 15 at Gus' Italian Café in Mechanicsville; I was hired as a dishwasher, making $4.35 an hour. It was my first taste of freedom and ability to have money, so I was all about it. I worked as often as I could so I could buy the things I wanted, like a bike, shoes, jeans, and eventually a crappy 1986 Ford Mustang car to drive when I turned 16. Despite me quitting the job early on, to go to a Charlie Daniels concert with backstage passes, the café owner, Scott, was incredibly trusting and provided me with a chance to excel. It didn't take long for me to acquire the skills to bus tables, cook, serve tables. I don't know why he trusted me so much at a young age but I'm thankful that he did. Eventually Scott gave me a key to the restaurant to open and close it on my own. The team at Gus' was like a second (and more fun) family. I loved them and worked there for six years.

Shortly after I was hired, a boy named Charlie was hired to work there. Voila, my work crush had arrived. Charlie was two years older than I was. Lordy, was he cute. Charlie was of Italian descent, shorter than me (but everyone was), brown hair and eyes, and smooth tanned skin. He was funny, confident, and didn't take himself that seriously. Charlie was hired as a dishwasher and he had no hesitations when it came to diving into the nasty drainage system. As he worked, I would steal glances at his cute butt – quickly enough that I would not get caught staring at him. I hoped in vain to catch a vibe that Charlie thought similarly. But there was no response.

During my senior year, I did end up with a girlfriend. Shannon was the daughter of a local minister. She was tall with long brown hair and brown eyes. Our relationship consisted of double dates with a friend of mine and a friend of hers who were also dating. We dated for a few months. I wasn't innately attracted to her like I was the boys but with raging hormones I had no problem when it came to making out and PG-13 type frolicking. I genuinely cared for her and hoped to eventually have sex with her to drop the virgin label but knew it wasn't likely due to her faith.

While dating Shannon, I couldn't take my eyes off a tall, blond-haired junior student named Shaun. Every morning while congregating with my friends, I would watch him from afar. He seemed shy, never had a girl hanging around, and wasn't part of any one school clique, which I liked. Shaun became my senior year crush.

I could not act on my interests; but I arranged to get closer to him by joining the track team since he was on it. I signed up to run cross-country, since that's what Shaun was doing. But it didn't allow for much conversation since people ran at different paces. I was so terrified to break the ice with him and risk being outed to the school, so I never introduced myself. I settled for admiring him while we stretched and ensuring to run behind him on the trails. Once my class graduated in June, I never saw him again.

I was intent on becoming a history teacher and I decided to follow Shannon to Longwood College, in Farmville, Virginia in the fall, since it was known as a great teacher's college. My relationship with Shannon didn't make it through the summer after high school. We broke up over religion, as she wanted me to attend Baptist church services more often and I disagreed. Prior to Shannon, I had been accepted into Radford University and planned to go there in the fall with a close friend of mine, Jeff, but by the time Shannon and I broke up, it was too late to change course and attend Radford with Jeff. I felt guilty and badly about it, as we were the only two in our circle of friends who had decided to go to college and now, we would both be flying solo at our respective colleges.

Around the time I graduated high school in 1998, the Internet was growing and computers for home use were reasonably priced.

With the money I received from Pap for graduation, I dumped $2,300 into a Packard Bell desktop computer and bought a different car. With a home computer, I could now venture online to explore my sexuality. Granted, it was at a ridiculously slow dial-up speed on AOL, but it was pure heaven to explore the gay chat rooms and find likeminded individuals. The only downside was obtaining the AOL CDs and ensuring you didn't go over your allotted hours before having to use a new disc. I remember the joy of finding nude images, but then the terror as they would download pixel by pixel—and I would panic that family members could walk in. I never met anyone online, but It was fun to talk to other deeply closeted people. I was only caught once, when one of my brothers, Rob, was in the room and noticed a gay softcore porn page on the screen. Naturally, I blamed it on Hollywood and that ended the issue.

That summer between high school and college was filled with trips to Virginia Beach and the Outer Banks of North Carolina with my close friends, Karl, Jeff, and Bob. We'd volunteer to work the evening shift at Gus' so we could wake up early and drive ninety minutes to the beach, spend the day in the sun and surf, and be back in time for the dinner rush. It had become normal for us to rent a beach house for a week in North Carolina where we would spend it trying to obtain alcohol, getting thrown off of go-kart tracks, or cruising around the beach town in our cars. At the end of the summer, I carried that behemoth computer with me in the back seat of the blue 1989 IROC-Z and off to college I went. By now, there was high-speed Internet, which increased my porn viewing pleasure. It was amazing to have endless porn at my fingertips. At the time, I was repulsed by hardcore porn and would stick to looking at photos of European twinks and videos of guys performing oral sex. I wasn't ready to view full on sex quite yet, it was a gradual process for me. I can't recall just how many trips I'd have to make down to the bathroom to take care of business, but my dorm roommate must've thought I had IBS. I'm shocked the college didn't intervene and shut down my connection.

Even while at college, I would drive home on weekends and continued working at Gus' Café. Charlie also worked there sporadically. I saw him a lot, since we both went to Longwood College and he would also come home on weekends to work there. He was into theatre and since I was in Bye Bye Birdie during my senior year of high school, I took a theatre class at Longwood as well, but we rarely saw each other on campus since he was always with his best friend and they were juniors in college. Gus' had a bar on one side and on Wednesdays and Saturdays there was karaoke. I had popped my karaoke cherry at a dive bar in Lewisville during a trip with Karl to Texas that previous summer. Once I did that, I knew I had the ability to do it at Gus' – but it was easier singing off-key in front of strangers.

But I worked up the courage to do karaoke at any opportunity I could while working at Gus'. I would get off of work, drive home to shower and change, then return in appropriate country attire to sing. I'd belt out George Strait, John Michael Montgomery, Clint Black, and Mark Chestnut like I was at the Academy of Country Music awards. I loved it and the audience reaction reaffirmed my desire to be a country music artist. My love for music had grown since listening to Mom's 8-Track tapes in her Camaro. I had amassed a collection of country tapes and CDs. I devoured the

George Strait CD box set, committing every song to memory and attempting a few on the guitar. I sang any chance I could and soon I decided that singing country music was all I ever wanted to do.

Coincidentally, Charlie's best friend was a guy named Jason. He was a nice guy who also came to Gus' to sing karaoke—except Jason brought the house down every freaking time. He was a fantastic singer. When Charlie was diagnosed with leukemia in 1999, his friend Jason wrote a song for his friend, calling it "The Remedy." Yes, Charlie's friend grew up to be musical star Jason Mraz. Charlie survived his leukemia and is married and works part-time at Gus' these days when he isn't focused on his small business.

I felt lost at Longwood College that fall. I didn't have the friends from high school or back home, classes were harder than I thought, and I was uncertain who I really was or who I wanted to present to the world. Some days I would wear cowboy boots and a cowboy hat to class, other days I dressed like everyone else. College was supposed to be this liberating place where you can reinvent yourself, or be who you truly want to be, but I didn't know who I really was. I spent a lot of time in my dorm room chatting on AOL instant messenger with friends back home. I didn't know why I was in college, as I had no real direction. My only goal was to play the acoustic guitar I'd purchased and become a country singer. I wanted to be the guy on the steps to the dorm playing guitar while people watched and admired, yet I lacked the confidence to actually do it. My grades were terrible, but the boys were cute. I was in a whole new place where nobody knew me, yet I was still afraid to do anything more than admire guys from afar and gorge myself on porn in my dorm. My roommate was from Boone, North Carolina, with a heavy accent, and I was afraid he'd find out I was gay and ridicule me. He was a great roommate and may have not cared at all, but the fear was enough to suppress all of it.

One evening in the dining hall while with guys from my floor, I began talking with a cute guy. He was a short and athletic guy with fair skin and lived on the floor above mine. We started talking about games we had on our computers. He asked if we could go back to my dorm to play them. I was unsure if he meant actually play the computer games or play with each other and got scared out of my mind. I guess I missed my first real opportunity, as he soon got up and left.

I ended up withdrawing from college after one semester, in December 1998, and headed back home to try and figure out what I was going to do with my life. I felt like I was wasting money that I didn't have to pursue an unknown objective. I didn't receive any pushback from my family or friends. I figured I could resume my studies when the time was right. I went back to working at Gus' full-time while finding my way forward. In early 1999, I stopped by the naval recruitment center in town to see what they had to offer. There was an abundance of military members in my family and I knew they'd help me pay for college in the future as well as provide a sense of direction for me, or at least until I was more mature. I was so deeply closeted, being gay and in the Navy was never a concern and I assumed I would find others like me along the way. I took the military aptitude test and scored well enough that the Navy recruiters said I could go into any field I wanted. Motivated by the large bonuses, I decided to sign up for the Navy's submarine program, under the delayed entry program, allowing me more time at home prior to leaving for basic training. As my time grew nearer to formally enlist and take the oath, I was growing worried that I had been roped into a program I didn't want to be in and carried heavy commitments, all for larger bonus. I talked with a friend's father who was an Army recruiter. He told me the delayed entry program didn't hold any weight and I could easily back out of it, since I hadn't formally enlisted. I ended up not joining the Navy and sought better options for my future.

Around that same time in 1999, Mom sold her house and moved to Pennsylvania to be near Pap, fleeing because she feared Hollywood might return, whom she'd thrown out and had continued contacting her. I went along with her and Stacie after my disastrous first semester at Longwood College since I had no idea what I was doing with my life at that point. Due to the pay differential, Mom kept her nursing job in Richmond and decided she would stay with a friend in Richmond for a week or two at a time while working double shifts and then return to Pennsylvania when she wasn't working. Since I was working at Gus' Café and was comfortable there, I decided to do the exact same thing, but on opposite weeks as Mom, so there was always someone there with Stacie in Pennsylvania, who was enrolled at school there. It was fantastic to be close to Pap, my father, grandparents, and other family members but I was bored while living there and had no social life since there wasn't one to be had. Mom bought an ATV, and I had a go kart, which were the main sources of entertainment while living there. My aunt and uncle were of great help during that time, helping cover any gaps there were when Mom or I were driving to and from Virginia for work and weren't in Pennsylvania. Mom's hiatus to Pennsylvania didn't last very long. She and Stacie moved back to Mechanicsville months later to start anew and where Mom's career could flourish while living in a new location that Hollywood was unaware of.

Between the ages of 18 and 20, I really began exploring my passion for country music. It seemed the only thing I could ever imagine myself doing. I wrote a few songs, mainly about feeling lost, missing home, and my starry-eyed desires to make it in Nashville. However, I didn't have the skill set to put any of them to music. I could listen to a song on the radio and write a whole new song to the melody but had no concept on marrying a new melody to my lyrics, so my songs piled up in a manilla folder. I was taking guitar lessons when I could afford it from the same teacher who had taught Jason Mraz, belting out karaoke at Gus' whenever I could, and trying to connect with anyone that could help.

When I was at Longwood, I had befriended Melina, a girl with an amazing voice. She had gone to Nashville to record a demo CD and played it for me. She had help from her family to get this accomplished. To me, it was badass. This was long before YouTube, social media, and iPhones. For some reason, that concept of recording a demo CD stuck in my head. I had my sister take photos of me looking all country with my guitar and truck, in case someone asked for them. After some AOL chat room querying, I was referred to a recording studio owner in Nashville. The guy said for $3,000 he could record a CD of me singing cover songs that I could send to radio stations to play. To my young brain, this sounded like a heck of a deal. I set out solo during the winter of 1999-2000 in my Chevy Blazer (the IROC was sold just before the engine electronics died) from Richmond and headed to Nashville. I'm still surprised Mom allowed me to do this. My trip also included a drive to Texas to look into Southwest Texas State University, where George

Strait had attended, with the thought of moving there to finish college and pursuing music. Learning the Texas country music circuit seemed like a logical step to success.

The drive was about twelve hours and seemed to take forever. But I made it and checked into a hotel close to Music Row. I was thrilled to be in the epicenter of country music, where dreams come true and my heroes made their work. The next day, the recording studio owner called. He was running late with another artist and our session would be delayed. The day wore on and it didn't appear we were going to meet. After some quick math, I realized I had not budgeted sufficient money to stay over another night. I knew I'd have to scrap the Texas leg of the trip and head back home before long. I found a country-western shop and bought a felt George Strait Stetson cowboy hat. Strait was my idol, for his genuine country roots, style, and class were everything I ever wanted to be as an artist. Then I headed back home.

I was disappointed in myself for underestimating how much the trip would cost and how ill-prepared I was. I had ample time on the drive to think about it. I'd hoped to return home with a CD in hand and a renewed sense of direction for my life. I knew I'd have to continue to find my way. A few months later, Jeff and I drove to Knoxville, Tennessee, to meet with an advisor from the University of Tennessee. Kenny Chesney had attended UT and given its proximity to Nashville, my young mind thought this might also be a good route to get back into college and pursue my country music aspirations. Jeff and I had a fun weekend in Knoxville but neither of us pursued it beyond that visit, the out of state tuition was too much for us to justify.

During this floundering time in my life, I received a $20,000 settlement from an insurance company. The award stemmed from a dog attack in middle school. The dog had bit half of my lip off, requiring plastic surgery to repair it. I had surgery at the time of the attack. But since I was young, I had the option to undergo additional treatment if I desired, once I was grown, if I didn't like how my lip looked. Or I could take the lump sum. As any impetuous young adult would do, I took the money, paid off credit card debt, and got into go-kart racing. A terrible investment that I enjoyed only one season before I sold everything. Outside of Gus', I bounced around in short-lived jobs, including Walmart, Ruby Tuesday, BB&T Bank, and commercial electrician apprentice. What followed were a few more car purchases.

Then I enlisted in the Virginia Air National Guard in April 2001. I needed some structure in my life. Given what Pap had done for the country and my uncle retiring from the Air Force, it seemed like the right decision. Mom was relieved I'd decided on some kind of direction for a change. Our family wasn't known for a lot of encouragement and emotional support. The belief was that after high school, the parents' job is done, and the kids need to figure the rest out.

I left for USAF basic training in July 2001 and headed to Lackland Air Force Base in San Antonio, Texas, during the hottest months of the year. Needless to say, it was quite the shock. I wasn't used to the early wakeups, constant observation, attention to detail, and I missed home. We were allowed one phone call a week which was very short, and you were being yelled at to "hurry up" by others waiting to use the phone. Basic Training sucked goat balls. There was a lot of boot polishing, a lot of marching, standing in formation, cleaning things that didn't need to be cleaned, pushups, running, and a lot of yelling. But by the third week, I realized that I could simply put my head down and get through it. I got used to the structure, 49-second group showers (nowhere near as erotic as it sounds), and even waking up at 2 AM to resolve the overnight erections. (Funny, a lot of guys used the bathroom overnight.) The best I could do was to steal glances at the guys I thought were cute but never risking a glace too long for fear of being thrown out of the military. Mostly, I did the best I could to not get yelled at.

Before I knew it, it was September 4, 2001 and we were in our final week. Somehow, we made Honor Flight, which made our drill sergeant very happy. That same week, he was picked up to be an Aerial Navigator as a lieutenant, so our final week was great. We got to eat from the revolving dessert case and had more time to consume our food. The mood was lighter. At the end of the week, he called us into the squad bay for a meeting. He started naming out airmen who were designated as Honor Graduates.

He called my name. I was floored by this announcement. It was the first time I'd been formally recognized by someone of authority.

I flew home on September 10, 2001, since I was in the split-op training program and would return to attend Air Force technical training at a later date. All I could think of was getting home and being able to sleep in for the first time in seven weeks.

I was awakened the next morning by my Nokia cellphone. Mom was telling me to turn on the TV. I watched in horror as the second tower was hit. Like all Americans, I was in shock. My next thought was "Holy fuck; I'm in the military" and this isn't what I'd signed up for. Not knowing what else to do, I put on my uniform and headed to my unit, the 192nd Fighter Wing in Richmond, VA. I got to the front gate and the guards were a little apprehensive, since I had literally just returned the day before, and I hadn't in-processed yet. I reported to my shop chief and asked what I needed to do. Unfortunately, I hadn't yet gone to technical school, so I wasn't of much help other than to keep things clean. But I felt better at least being there.

Most of the unit was immediately activated. As it turned out, our F-16s were the first ones in the air that day. I helped out where I could, but due to my training status, I was ineligible to go to the Middle East when my unit was deployed.

After a month of being home and on active-duty orders, reporting to base every day, I returned to working at Gus' and my jumble of part-time jobs. I worked in the area until I left for Air Force technical school training in November 2002. I was happy to be back on active duty and in the comforting structure of the military. I imagine these feelings are common among the ranks and why people stay in for as long as they do. I got to Sheppard Air Force Base in Wichita Falls, Texas. I was an Electrician and Environmental Specialist and we handled anything with wires running to it and the cabin pressurization and air-conditioning on Air Force aircraft, though my focus would be on fighter planes.

I luckily had some really good classmates. One was very cute, Adam. He never knew how much I adored him, since I kept it buried deep and played the standard friend role. Adam was tall and slender, had beautiful blue eyes and light brown hair, and looked good shirtless. In hindsight, we actually looked kind of similar. I admired him and hoped that we'd cross that line. For the first time, I began manscaping in hopes of it. Adam and I both came from smaller towns, had a similar sense of humor, similar taste in music, and neither of us ever talked in depth about women. There was an air of uncertainty between us, though it never got in the way of hanging out after class, but it was enough to question if he was feeling the same way I was. Our class was stuck together for about six months, so it helped that we all got along, as the program was challenging.

In the first few weeks there, I volunteered to be a student leader for our squadron, as I was emboldened by my honor graduate ribbon in basic training to step up. During training, the sergeants would enlist the help of students for positions of leadership. Those students were assigned a colored rope that was worn over the right shoulder of the uniform. The rope colors were green, yellow, and red, with graduating levels of responsibility. I was a green rope for a few weeks and then a yellow rope for the remainder of our training, since I botched my interview with the squadron sergeant for a red rope. While marching in formation, I enjoyed being out to the side, calling the tempo and pace of the march for the squadron and seeing what it was like to be in a leadership role. It didn't seem to affect the relationships with my classmates, as we usually had a great time after hours.

There were three us who hung out together constantly: Josh, Adam, and I. I was all about some Adam. Since there weren't many females to be found, I didn't have to feign interest in them to keep up the façade.

As the months passed, Adam and I never crossed that line nor did it even get close. I never let my attraction to Adam get in the way of doing well in the program and ensuring we all progressed as a team. It was agonizing to desire this man I spent so much time with, and yet being unable to act on it. I spent many hours fantasizing what it would be like to be romantically involved with him—or simply to be able to gaze into his eyes. But I had to settle for being a friend and classmate. Our only contact was the accidental brushing of arms. I was afraid of rejection, afraid of ruining a friendship, afraid of being kicked out of the military.

I remained in my shell the entire time.

We graduated from training in April 2003 and I headed back to Richmond. For months after that I struggled with joining the Air Force full time or remaining as a reservist; I missed the comradery, the structure, the steady paychecks, and Adam most of all. I'd developed more feelings for him than I'd realized, and it took me a while to come to terms with the reality that we were on two different paths. To go active duty in hopes of getting to North Dakota, where Adam was, without him even knowing how I felt, seemed like a long shot.

I was back home. After another month-long stint of training for the Air Force in Clovis, New Mexico in July 2003, I re-enrolled at Longwood University. It was time to complete my degree since the military was now footing the bill. I set my sights on Criminal Justice and had a better idea of where I wanted my path to lead. Since I'd done so well in the military environment, it made sense that law enforcement would be a logical direction. My great-grandfather had been a sheriff and I had an uncle that was a Pennsylvania State Trooper, so I figured it ran in the family. I applied with the Hanover County Sheriff's Office and Henrico County Police Department in the fall of 2003 while at Longwood, and I was progressing in their hiring processes. I had begun running and working out on a regular basis to prepare for what may lay ahead. I was doing well in my classes for a change and had a fantastic advisor-professor who made learning interesting. Dr. Kelley was a middle-aged college professor and enthusiastic. I enjoyed her classes and was highly interested in sociology and the economic aspect of Criminal Justice. For the first time in a while, I felt as though things were finally on track and I'd be the first in my family to obtain a bachelor's degree.

In December 2003, I received an offer of employment with Hanover County with a salary of $32,000. it coincided with the end of the semester. I was 24 at the time, so I felt it was time to get the career ball rolling. I accepted the position, finished the semester, and left Longwood.

After joining the Hanover Sheriff's Office, the first thing I did with this new paycheck was buy a truck. The 2004 Nissan Frontier 4x4 off-road version was my first new vehicle purchase. I knew I'd have a take-home police cruiser and gas was way cheaper back then. I had a month to wait until police academy started, so I joined other recruits (eloquently known as FNGs—fucking new guys) in menial tasks. But we also got to do some ride-along with officers.

One day, we responded to a bank robbery in Mechanicsville. While the officer was assisting, I set my coffee on the dashboard in the patrol car. Just then, a priority call for service came in. As we backed out of the bank, my coffee fell into the officer's lap. That call was a heated domestic involving a weapon, with children present, one of which was on the phone with dispatch. We could hear the screams for help, and we got there as fast as we could,

We arrived right behind another unit. The small children were at the front door, still holding the phone. Their father, the male suspect, was in the rear of the house, his hands covered in blood, and was immediately handcuffed. On the kitchen floor lay his wife, lifeless. The pool of blood on the kitchen floor was immense, as the suspect had attempted to cut her head off. The smell of the blood and gore permeated the house. I still recall that smell, over fifteen years later.

When I got to my apartment that night, my roommate Michelle knew something had happened and we talked about it at length. I hadn't ever witnessed death like that before and felt I needed to talk to someone about it. I wasn't distraught but was definitely disturbed by the night's events. I felt better after we talked, she helped put my mind at ease that it's an unfortunate part of the job and will be a rare one. I knew if I could handle that type of situation and maintain my composure, I'd be okay in the line of work.

I wasn't sure what to expect during the police academy, but I prepared for the worst, thinking it'd be a repeat of military basic training. It wasn't. There wasn't any yelling and screaming. We drove to and from the academy daily, had lunch breaks, and were treated like adults. In our class, top graduates received a brand-new police cruiser and remaining members got beat-up older models. In policing, a new patrol car ranks very high on the list of morale boosters. I came in second place overall. While I disputed my test result, I received an old beater, car number 160. I still took pride in the mustard-striped Crown Vic and waxed it the first day I got it home. We were taught the importance of appearance: If you showed up at a crime scene and looked polished, composed, and confident, it would prevent confrontations from occurring. There was a study done on cop killers. One of the takeaways was that the killers all said that the officer they attacked looked sloppy. I took that advice to heart. My uniforms were always pressed, shoes always clean, and my car was most definitely clean.

Field training consisted of a month on each shift, riding with an assigned field training officer. We were thrown into varying tasks until you could handle yourself. We operated as solo officers on an assigned beat. My first training officer was great but a little too laidback. He was very competent and had a way with putting citizens at ease with his personality and humor, but I felt uncoordinated and sloppy in how I handled calls; I was lacking a method. My second training officer, on midnight shift, was knowledgeable and traffic-oriented. But since it was midnight shift, he would have me pull over somewhere around 3 AM and sleep. Meanwhile, I'm a paranoid new guy, afraid of sleeping on duty or being murdered by someone. So I would sit there in a panic until he woke up just in time for dayshift roll-call. That officer was a member of the crash team, who are officers trained in the science of car crashes and how to reconstruct them, usually when a fatality occurs during a car crash. It was fascinating to watch and hear first-hand how a crash and fatality occurred. During my month with him, I responded to any fatality car crash any chance I could.

My final and most important training officer was on dayshift. I was assigned to a retired Army guy from New Jersey who took up policing as his retirement gig. We got along very well, as he was personable and fun to ride around with. I learned the most from him, as he helped me create a system and he was phenomenal when dealing with the public. He could calm a heated situation with his pragmatic approach to policing, while maintaining his composure at all times.

I was formally released from field training in the normal amount of time and assigned to dayshift as unit 124. In Hanover County, there's the east end and west end of the county. The east end is much closer to the City of Richmond and is far more populated than the more rural west end. The new guys and proactive guys all wanted to work the east end for the higher call volume and ability to find things to do. I was tossed to the central and west side of the county since I was new. I drove around uneventfully in those first six months.

The caveat to being in the west side of the county was when you did get calls for service, it was usually more heated by the time you arrived on scene. Worse, your backup may be ten to thirty minutes away. That is an eternity when a cop is dealing with a heated domestic. People in the west end of the county usually waited longer to call the police for help, as they're more country and that's just how they roll. That's usually a bad thing for first responders. I survived dayshift without getting my ass handed to me and I took that as a win. I wanted to get on evening shift, where the real action was.

In April 2004, I was still roommates with Michelle when I got my first puppy. I bought a Jack Russell Terrier and named him Baxter. I had always wanted a dog of my own and now that I had a legit job, the timing was right. I wanted a high-energy dog that was smaller in size but could keep up with me on runs, and Baxter fit the bill perfectly. One day I came home from work and saw Baxter nibbling on an odd device in the middle of the living room floor. I realized it was Michelle's vibrator device, named the Rabbit, which Baxter had found under her bed. She was mortified but I thought it was hilarious.

Michelle was in shape and after shedding weight from her previous relationship, she gave the guys a run for their money and was a blast to live with. We were both playing the field in our early twenties. I was dating girls here and there, still hiding who I really was and obeying the rules of straight society – but generally enjoying life, even in the closet. I met my next girlfriend through a guy at the Virginia Air National Guard, as it was his stepdaughter. Tiffany was a great woman, but as the months passed, I didn't feel that innate sense that she was "the one." But alas, I stayed put in the relationship. We dated for a year and a half before I had enough. On nights when we weren't hanging out, I could be found hiding in my bedroom looking at men online and that's where my interests laid. I told her I just didn't feel that connection with her and broke things off.

In the summer of 2006, I was out for a night of fun with Michelle, her boyfriend, and his firefighter colleagues. One of the guys had parked his car at my place. Once we got back, he said he'd had too much to drink and asked to stay at my place. I was mildly attracted to him and had been watching him all evening. The guy didn't seem to be that drunk and we'd made extended eye contact multiple times during the night, so I figured he was using this excuse to stay the night at my apartment.

Once we were upstairs, it got awkward immediately as we discussed where he should sleep. I knew I wanted him to sleep with me and it seemed he felt the same way, but we both retreated from the notion and he slept on the sofa instead. I was again afraid I'd been misreading his cues and dreaded the rejection and the repercussions that would follow. I reminded myself that the consequences could include being outed and losing my job, neither of which I was prepared for. Michelle had stayed with her boyfriend that night and the next day, I casually mentioned the awkward situation to her to see what her reaction was. She was uncertain as to the other guys sexuality but didn't seem surprised by it, either. I laughed it off and avoided disclosing my own true feelings.

There were many evenings where I would drive around while on patrol or just park somewhere and turn my SiriusXM radio to the OutQ station. It was the only resource I had at the time and it was exciting to listen to Michelangelo Signorile or Derek and Romaine talk about a world I wanted to be a part of, a lot of which was totally foreign to me. After most shifts, I began spending more time online, interacting with other men in the Richmond area, outside of my county, and soon getting brave enough to exchange photos.

I finally had the nerve to meet up with a guy in July 2006. After all of this pent-up desire, for years, the time finally came. I met Andrew through a computer dating service. Andrew had straight fair hair, hazel eyes, smaller frame, a great smile, and was a couple of years younger than I was, making him a twink in gay terminology. I drove to his place in the west end of Richmond. I felt safer meeting up with someone who didn't live in the county I worked and lived. He greeted me at the door in a bathrobe. I was very nervous and didn't know how this was to play out. I was also fearful of my safety, given the horror stories of hookups gone awry.

I followed him to his bedroom. He was a sweet guy with a big penis, eight inches and thick. We fooled around a bit. Once we had both cleaned ourselves up, Andrew asked if I wanted to cuddle. That freaked me out. I wasn't ready for that kind of connection, which would have also meant admitting I was gay. I quickly put my clothes on and left. We ended up seeing each other again and I explained to him that he was my first male experience. Andrew seemed to understand.

Once that first time was finally behind me and Jesus didn't strike me with lightning, I knew I was actually attracted to guys. Now I felt I could take additional baby steps to explore my sexuality. At the time I was still living in the Mechanicsville apartment that I got when first hired by the Sheriff's Office. My friend, Jeff, had moved in and then moved out, after disputes over rent and employment. I had been chatting with a guy I met on Myspace (let's call him Sampson) during the summer of 2006. Sampson had lived in Henrico County, VA, but moved to D.C. for a job. His profile picture was captivating and drew me in, as the sun was reflecting in his brown eyes in contrast with a bright blue Abercrombie polo. He was handsome and had short brown hair and was five feet eight inches. He came across as confident and comfortable with himself, a trait I lacked. The conversations flowed well and we exchanged a few calls that year and kept in contact, despite his relocation. I felt I could carry on this relationship since it was contained online and there was no risk of friends, family, or coworkers finding out about him. When he called, I could easily step away from whatever I was doing to talk on my Motorola Razor, and nobody was the wiser. I was still deeply closeted and felt I would have more liberty to be myself if I moved to Henrico County, since it was more democratic and surely more populated with LGBTQ folks than Hanover County was. In October of 2006. I put a contract on a two-bedroom condo in the west end of Richmond, in the Laurel Lakes neighborhood. It was perfect for Baxter and me, as it had a massive green area and a large balcony. Besides, it wasn't far from the Hanover County line so I could still take my patrol car home every night. At the time, I was driving an obnoxiously loud 2004 Ford Mustang GT. I'd taken the catalytic converters off, installed a short throw shifter, and made a few other modifications so I could take it to Richmond Dragway for fun. Jeff and Josh, another close high school friend, were also into modifying their cars and racing them at the dragstrip and is usually where we could be found on fall evenings.

In the fall of 2006, I went back to school to complete my bachelor's degree that I'd started a few times. I was comfortable in my role as a police officer and felt I could now handle the additional work required to complete my degree. I had always felt as though I let myself down and felt inferior to those who had completed their degrees. I wanted to prove to myself, my family, and set an example for my future children.

A peer at the Sheriff's Office was taking classes at Bluefield College's Richmond campus. He gave me the contact of someone at the school for more information. They offered classes at night and the Sheriff's Office offered education leave, which could be used during your shift, in addition to being able to drive the patrol car to and from class. I attended an informational seminar and enrolled in the program as a full-time student in the criminal justice program for the fall 2006 semester. I attended classes two nights a week. At times, I'd begin my shift on patrol, leave for a few hours to attend class, and then return to duty. I did this for a year and a half and made the Dean's list and President's list for the first time in my educational career—while also working full time. I enjoyed the studies and it came a little easier to me this time.

Sampson ended up moving back to Richmond in the fall of 2006 as well. That November, we finally met in person for the first time. I picked him up at his place in my redneck Mustang and we went to Panera for lunch in Virginia Center Commons. He was living with his best friend Doug, across the street from the condo I was closing on two weeks later. He was ridiculously cute, wearing the bright blue Abercrombie polo I'd seen in his online profile months prior. The lunch went well, so we continued talking.

I closed on the condo, my first home purchase, in mid-December 2006 and I was ecstatic to be a homeowner—and out of Hanover County. I felt as though I could begin to warm into my own skin with less fear of a hate crime, shame, or risk of losing my job. In Virginia, it's a "right to work" state where you could be fired for any given reason. Being that I worked for a Sheriff's Office in a red county, it was inherently political. It was best that I live beyond the county border if I were to further explore my sexuality. The people I'd grown up around and those I worked with were great people. But that doesn't always mean they were open-minded. I felt strongly enough about protecting myself to avoid those situations. Besides, I'd heard my direct supervisor at the sheriff's office use the term "faggot" one day during roll call, so I didn't exactly get warm and fuzzy feelings.

In Henrico County in my new home, I was beginning to feel more comfortable. The odds of running into someone I knew was lower and I felt I could live more anonymously and without fear of judgement. My neighbors minded their own business and I was free to have Sampson over any time I liked. It was liberating to have that autonomy. I loved having my own condo and Baxter seemed equally content. I was saving money at a decent pace and was changing the condo's appearance to make it my own. When

I bought the condo, the entire thing was painted in a light beige color. It was clean but needed some color on the walls, new blinds for the windows, and updating to the kitchen by replacing the countertops and painting the cabinets. Sampson had great taste when it came to home décor and paint colors, so he had an influence in that department. We were spending lots of time together. We'd often go out to eat together, go to Busch Gardens theme park, browse car dealerships, shopping at the mall, coffee shops, or trips to Costco for their pizza and churros. I admired his collection of color-coded polos hanging in his closet, the way he meticulously cared for things he owned, his knowledge of cars, and his bachelor's degree hanging on his bedroom wall. He was smart and witty. He introduced me to music outside of the classic rock and country genres, possessing an equally large repertoire of CDs as I had.

In hindsight, I allowed him a little too much influence in my condo makeover. I spent a lot of money on a Natuzzi leather sectional and a contemporary European glass coffee table from La Diff, which were price-wise above what I was accustomed to. Sampson introduced me to Crate & Barrel, as he'd worked there part-time. He helped me to dress better, banishing the baggy clothes that hung off of me. I was learning a lot through Sampson and we were growing closer together. I gave him a key to my condo, and he was spending a lot more time at my place. When he wasn't at my place, we were across the street at he and Doug's townhome. Sampson and I were also exploring each other sexually. For the first time in my life, I bottomed and did not enjoy it whatsoever but thankfully I was face down and hid the grimace from Sampson. I wanted to be a good boyfriend and show I wasn't THAT conservative or selfish.

Sampson still lived with Doug, whom he had dated, a couple of years prior to our meeting. This was an odd concept to me, coming from the straight world, and wasn't easy to digest. It took a lot of time to accept their relationship. Too often I felt like the third wheel. I was jealous of their relationship and at times, I felt like I had to compete with Doug to make Sampson laugh or for his attention. Doug was successful, funny, out, and smart. A tall order to compete with. When we would go to the mall, they walked so fast and got along so well, I would often walk behind them or jump into the backseat of the car, participating in conversations whenever I fully heard what was being discussed. I was also envious of their educational achievements since I hadn't completed my degree yet and it made me feel inferior at times. I wondered how I was supposed to compete with someone who had an MBA, owned a nice townhome, and made significantly more than I did.

In early 2007, I was working evening shift and heard a call for a motor vehicle accident along Route 360. heading towards King William County. I was on the complete opposite end of Route 360, so I wasn't a responding officer. A coworker suddenly requested that I switch to another radio channel. I was alerted that my sister Stacie had been involved in the accident. My presence was requested at the scene. I was shaking and ran code 3 (lights and siren) across that part of the county, a long stretch. When I arrived on scene, my sister's Mustang was in the swamp. Thankfully, she and my baby niece Gracie were unharmed.

Shortly thereafter, I told Sampson what had occurred, and we discussed our thoughts on having a family. The accident left me shaken, at how easily I could have lost my sister or niece. I had always known I wanted to be a father, but Sampson admitted he didn't want to have children. That was enough to end the relationship. I couldn't see my life without having children some day and as we sat on the living room floor of my condo, it was a divide I couldn't overcome and thought it best we stop dating. He grabbed a few things he had at my place and left the condo. I cried for a bit but picked myself up and refocused on work.

Meanwhile, at the Sheriff's Office, I was having a blast. I was on evening shift and was gaining experience. I had been assigned to patrol the east end of the county. I loved the hours, my coworkers, the call volume, the tempo of the shift, traffic stops, and the ability to get into criminal work more easily. The camaraderie was what I had been seeking since the Air Force. I knew the officers who worked beside me better than my actual brothers. That's a plus when you find yourself in heated situations. You need to know how to read the other officers without saying a word. Your life depends on one another.

You know your beat partners' situation by the tone of their voice on the radio. One listen and you know whether they are calm, in control, or stressed in a bad situation and relying on you to help as fast as possible. At times, it was bloodcurdling to hear your peer needing help, not knowing what was transpiring. Meanwhile, you were driving as fast as you can through traffic. I'd been in those moments, driving well above speed limits to help your partner in danger. It took me some time, but I eventually learned to think beyond the crime scene itself when responding to a call and take into account time delays in 911 calls, exit routes for suspects, and potential destinations.

I'll admit, it was fun chasing cars into Henrico County and the

City of Richmond (where most of the pursuits went). You went from calm and collected to full of adrenaline in a matter of seconds and it was exhilarating. Foot pursuits were also fun, as I'm tall and lean so running comes naturally. Back in my twenties, jumping over fences and tackling suspects came a lot easier – even wearing twenty lbs. of gear. It was gratifying.

Around 2007, I started prepping to be a field training officer (an officer who trains new officers upon graduating from the police academy) for the department. I had always enjoyed teaching and was happy the supervisors felt confident that I could train new officers. I got certified to train the recruits, teach firearms, and be a general instructor for the regional police academy. I thoroughly enjoying teaching the classes, teaching at the gun range, and, most importantly, on the street, where it all came together. I loved to see that a-ha moment in a trainee when the lessons all came together for them. There was also the perk of seeing who we were hiring and having a say in their training, prior to being released as a solo officer. (I was also curious to see if we hired any cute ones, for ogling purposes only.)

I had been concurrently conducting background investigations as well but being more involved in the training process was more fitting for me. Sometimes I would recommend to not hire an applicant, but he was hired anyway due to his ties with the higher-ups. One of these guys I warned about, months later, lost his temper and threw his flashlight at a passing vehicle. He was fired. They can't say I didn't warn them.

Once the department figured out that I was competent, I was inundated with new recruits. The most I had in a year was six, but

I was getting burnt out by it. Sometimes you just want solitude in your own police car. One of the recruits that year was absurdly attractive. He had a great smile, blond hair, and gorgeous blue eyes. I had no issue with this kind, sweet, and smart man being in the car for a month. Normally I didn't favor blonds, but he was an exception. And I couldn't figure out if he was gay or straight. His body language, his meticulous appearance, his eye contact, and coy smile drove me nuts. But I was still in the closet at work and didn't dare cross any lines. I wouldn't sacrifice my integrity, reputation, and honor; they were paramount to my success.

In the spring of 2007, Sampson and I began talking again via text message. We reconciled our differences from the break-up a few months prior. I felt as though I had overreacted in breaking things off with him, following my sister Stacie's car crash and I had convinced myself that Sampson was worth trying to work through things. I had grown to really like him, and he'd introduced me to a lot of the Richmond gay community that helped me start living more confidently as a gay man. He was sweet and I felt that time may change his thoughts on children, since it wasn't in the immediate future anyhow.

I recall one regret while field training. I got myself and a recruit into a hairy situation. We were working in the east end and responded to a call for a man with a gun in a residential area. We'd parked on an adjacent street, as two other units were already at the man's house. I was attempting to covertly approach the subject from behind, as he'd moved out into the driveway. As any officer knows, situations are fluid and everchanging. I decided to low-crawl (Army style) behind a small fence in the yard across from the subject's house. As I was halfway to a large tree that would serve as a great shield, I looked back. Alarmingly, my recruit was doing the same, disobeying my request that he stay in place—except he was as big as a house and I was thin. That fence isn't tall enough to cover that mammoth man, who looked like a bear in a cop uniform. Then the armed man began walking in our direction and I couldn't see him. All I could hear were his footsteps and I was a wide-open target. My stomach dropped. Honestly, I don't think I'd felt more perilous than at that moment. Thankfully, the two other units were able to coerce the man back towards his own driveway. I jumped up and ran for the nearest tree for cover. I moved in behind him and the subject was eventually was taken into custody.

A few other dangerous situations stand out to me. One evening, I was walking around a low-income apartment community, where I had lived two decades earlier. I had parked my patrol car out of view and was simply walking around, talking to residents. As I approached the building I had once lived in, a resident alerted me to a group of males gathered around an SUV nearby and insisted a gun was involved. I was on foot patrol by myself at the time and radioed for assistance as I approached the vehicle. I caught the group of four off-guard, and it was immediately apparent something was afoot. Police often talk about a sixth sense when you know something isn't right—and this was one of those moments.

As I asked what they were up to, one of them began reaching into his pocket. I immediately drew down on him. The younger one, a juvenile, was wise enough to pull his hand from his pocket and place them on the vehicle, as instructed. One of the other males in the group began to walk to the other side of the SUV, where I couldn't see him. I yelled to tell him to stop. So now I had four men at gunpoint, possibly armed, by myself, and my police car wasn't close by, meaning my colleagues who were responding to me couldn't easily find me, nor could I give details over the radio. It was a shitty situation. But I thanked God for a couple of things that I learned later: The guy on the other side of the SUV, who I stopped, was reaching for a gun on the driver's seat. The juvenile didn't pull the black metal BB gun from his pocket. The last thing any police officer wants to do is use lethal force on anyone, despite the high-profile police shootings that have dominated the news in recent years.

Another situation involved a suicidal woman with a gun. I was eating dinner at Arby's, since they gave police officers fifty-percent discounts on meals. The manager was gay, about my age, and liked me, so I enjoyed eating there even if it was just to be flirtatious with the manager. A call came out from a dispatcher for a heated dispute in the next beat over, which was fairly close by. A couple of neighboring beat officers said they'd report to the dispute and find out what was going on, since they knew I was trying to eat. But after hearing that a gun was involved, I dropped dinner and responded. As I was on the way, the officers at the house reported that a shot had been fired inside of the residence and the situation was still unfolding. Upon arriving to the house, I saw a woman standing in the driveway, holding a gun to her chest.

I angled myself in a safe position and one in which I wouldn't accidentally shoot my peers, as there were now three of us with weapons pointed at this woman. We were always taught that someone who is suicidal is also homicidal. That is, their mental state is one in which they aren't valuing their own life, so they also won't value yours. We spent some time trying to convince her to drop the gun. Without warning, she shot herself in the upper chest.

Though I had seen myriad crime scenes through the years, I hadn't yet witnessed someone shoot themselves in front of me. In the movies, people who are shot instantly fall over and die, but not in real life. It seemed an eternity before she tossed the gun a few feet in front of her. She stood there for a bit and then collapsed to the ground. I learned later that the bullet had gone right through her heart—and that the victim had been a clinical trauma nurse. It was a surreal thing to experience and my mind didn't begin to process it until days later. The department had us meet with the psychiatrist to make sure we were coping with the situation properly, but it was more of a formality than anything. In the machismo world of law enforcement, meeting as a group with the psychiatrist and admitting to having difficulty processing a death could be seen as a weakness and wasn't the best way to approach it. My mind replayed the events of that night repeatedly and it remains a memory scorched into my mind. Death is always a tragedy and to see it occur in front of you, when it was preventable, makes you realize how fragile and fleeting life really is.

A few months later, at our annual awards ceremony, the officers who handled the suicide were awarded the Sheriff's Office Silver Star Award for bravery. I was included. I was perplexed by this, as we just happened to be on patrol that night and responded to a very unfortunate situation. I felt like they'd given us awards for not shooting her. It was a no-win situation we found ourselves in and, if anything, I hoped important lessons would be learned from it.

We had some stellar supervisors on evening shift, particularly the sergeants who worked the east end of the county. You wanted to be a better officer because of them and emulate their style of leadership. They also made working fun. They were there when you needed them, always available to answer questions or resolve a complex problem if you couldn't, while never belittling or managing in a condescending manner. As long as you were productive, competent, and looked out for your peers, you were given the liberty we all sought.

One fall we had a string of vandalisms. Somebody was coming repeatedly to a Nissan dealership in Mechanicsville at night and slashing the tires on new cars. The dealership was in my assigned area and prior attempts to catch the suspect had been fruitless. One evening I decided to set up at the dealership after-hours. I parked my patrol car amongst the Nissans in the back area, where the cars had been getting vandalized.

I was doing some schoolwork when I heard rustling in the wooded area behind the dealership. Out of the woods popped this middle-aged white guy. Seconds later, I heard air escaping from tires. I was in disbelief that this jackass had no idea I was sitting there. I quietly notified dispatch what was transpiring, then got out of my car. I made my way towards the perp in between vehicles and drew down on him, as he was holding a sizable knife. He was utterly shocked to see me, as he was caught in the act. He tossed the knife into the woods, then complied with my commands to go face-first on the ground, so I could put him in handcuffs. Shortly thereafter, I was awarded the Sheriff's Office silver challenge coin for outstanding police work. But I was just doing my job.

The Sheriff's Office permitted citizens to do a ride-along with patrol officers. These could be attendees or graduates of the citizens police academy, students in criminal justice, or normal citizens who have an interest, Sometimes I'd get an older citizen or someone who didn't have great communication skills. That meant I was stuck with this person for nine hours. However, it could be an absolute blast if you knew the ride-along.

One evening, my boyfriend Sampson did a ride along during a busy evening. I was working the east end of the county and hopping from call to call. There was a motor vehicle accident along Route 360—in the "flats," a long, straight section of the highway between Hanover County and King William County. It's where people tended to speed, and where my sister had crashed. The dispatch reported it was a serious accident and I should get there as soon as possible. We were in the downtown area of Mechanicsville, so we kicked it into high gear, running code 3. We found a large jacked-up pickup truck on its side along the side of the highway. A driver was hanging halfway out of it. Sampson was shocked by the sight. The driver was pronounced dead on scene. We shut the roadway down, secured the scene, and waited for the crash team to arrive. Their job was to reconstruct the accident and figure out what happened.

Chapter Four

In April 2007, my enlistment was up in the Virginia Air National Guard and I was uncertain what I was going to do; I'd always wanted to be an officer in the military and my bachelor's degree, that I'd resumed working on, was nearing completion. A bachelor's degree is required to get a commission and become an officer in the military. My unit, the 192nd Fighter Wing, was home to a squadron of F-16s and there wasn't an abundance of officer spots available. I preferred to get a direct commission and attend the "meet-and-greet" officer boot camp, due to my blooming law enforcement career, instead of the longer traditional officer boot camp. A peer in the electric shop where I worked had been accepted into the Air Force active-duty pilot training program, so I knew it was possible. But I no longer wished to be on active duty. I had grown tired of working on airplanes. To cross-train would've required another lengthy stint at Sheppard Air Force Base in Wichita Falls, Texas.

I ended up reenlisting for another four years in the same position, since I was now a Staff Sergeant and knew what I was doing when it came to working on the F-16. Plus, the $20,000 reenlistment bonus they offered me was hard to pass up since I had condo maintenance expenses.

In July 2007, I went on a guys' trip to the Outer Banks of North Carolina with some close friends, only three hours from Richmond. One afternoon while drinking on the beach, we were being foolish 20-something males and began wrestling (I guess to prove masculinity). I ran up behind the one I was attracted to and attempted to take him down. He came down on top of my left leg. I felt a slight electrical jolt. Being buzzed, I attempted to walk it off, though it hurt like hell. Later my leg was noticeably swollen, so my childhood best friend, Karl, took me to the nearest emergency room. An x-ray confirmed I'd broken my leg. They placed it in a semi-cast, enough to stabilize my leg until I got back to Richmond for a proper cast. This was a sobering moment in more than one way, as a break could endanger my career. From the beach, I called my sergeant to tell him what occurred. I was embarrassed for acting like an idiot, which now impacted the other officers on my shift. Upon returning to work, I was placed on light duty for a few months until my leg was healed and I could return to patrol. That was the last time I drunk-wrestled.

As 2007 progressed, there was growing concern that the Department of Defense Base Realignment and Closure Committee (BRAC) was targeting our unit for closure in the near future. We hoped that we would not be affected, due to our proximity to Washington, D.C. I had just reenlisted which added additional concern as to how they'd handle folks like me. Supposedly, the Department of Defense was listening to a congressman who was lobbying to close our unit and consolidate the Langley Air Force Base squadrons. His push was successful; our unit would close down within a year. Even worse, our F-16s were being sent to other Air National Guard units and the job that I had been doing for the last six years didn't exist on the more advanced F-22 jets. I was given the option to stay in the guard, requiring me to retrain into a new job field that required nine months of training—or I could leave the Air National Guard. If I left, I would be able to keep the reenlistment bonus.

Sampson wasn't a big fan of me being in the reserves due to the chance of deployment. He never gave me a hard time about being in the reserves or the weekends I spent in uniform, but I understood his perspective. He dating somebody who went to work every day with the risk of danger. He also had to deal with the possibility I'd be deployed to the Middle East as well. I wanted to prioritize Sampson and prove it with actions, not just words. Couple all of that with my desire to be commissioned in the military, and my bachelor's degree nearly complete, I opted to leave the Air National Guard in October 2007.

It was bittersweet, as I enjoyed the people that I worked with and doing something different one weekend a month, setting myself apart from my peers. However, a sense of guilt was felt as I left the Air National Guard. In the time since 9/11, I had never been deployed to the Middle East, unlike much of the active-duty components of the military. I felt as though I hadn't sacrificed like others I knew. It's led to me to downplay my time in the military and view my time there as barely serving. The Guard had provided me with some invaluable life experience, as I fully believe I landed the job with the Sheriff's Office due to my Guard experience. The military helped instill some badly needed life discipline, as well as skills in organization, leadership, and teamwork—not to mention financial assistance with the GI Bill and tuition when I was a full-time student. Like they do in Taiwan, I believe people coming out of high school should be required to serve a year or two in one of the reserve components or in a similar organization to learn valuable life skill sets. I know that I was bumbling around aimlessly until I joined the military and certainly wouldn't be where I am today without that experience.

A couple of months after leaving the Air National Guard, in December 2007, I finally graduated with my bachelor's degree in criminal justice from Bluefield College. After nine years of attending different colleges, taking classes during summer sessions, juggling the demands of shift work, and finding ways to pay for it, the elusive degree was finally mine. I was quite proud, as the only member of my family to hold a bachelor's degree and without outside support or guidance. I'd always been envious of Sampson's degree, displayed on his wall, and now I was part of the club. I had higher aspirations than just working at the Sheriff's Office and the degree was the key that would open doors for me.

Sampson and I attempted to live together in early 2008. He had been slowly bringing things over, had a key to the condo, and even purchased a piece of furniture for the place. It felt like a big step for us and I hoped it would lower my insecurities that existed because of his relationship with Doug. But that didn't work out very well, probably because of how rigid I was in how I kept my condo. Everything in my condo had its proper place, even the bedroom that subbed as an office. Sampson didn't feel as though the condo was his home. He wasn't a dog person, either, which was another issue of contention between us, as I allowed Baxter to have full reign of the condo. Sampson moved out after a couple of months, back in with Doug.

I ignored the warning signs and kept trying to keep Sampson happy, since I enjoyed being with him. He was attractive, he was family oriented, and we shared a lot of common interests. To that point, he had been the only guy I'd ever dated. I was uncertain how relationships worked in the gay world and I did what I thought I was supposed to do. When we hung out, it was often with Doug. Together, Sampson and Doug could be cynical but when they were, I ignored it and sat quietly. I liked Doug as well, as a person and friend, but the dynamic between them added a barrier that was difficult for me to overcome.

The Richmond gay world accepted me quickly and people were genuinely nice, as Southern hospitality dictates. Granted, as any newcomer and a cop, I attracted a lot of attention. The scene was puzzling; there seemed to be two separate camps. One was the established older gays, around my age and up. The other folks differed from the established gays. They were fresh out of college or in retail or hospitality careers. I was dumbfounded how these two circles wouldn't socialize with each other, even as a minority group. I had imagined one big homogenous family, but those ideals were only in my head.

It seemed the established gays considered themselves to be the A-listers of Richmond. Many of them did have great jobs, lovely homes, and great social gatherings. I was able to be a part of both groups and met lots of nice people. I enjoyed hanging out with the younger, down-to-earth crowd, as they seemed more genuine and weren't out to prove anything.

It was a great feeling to be myself, even if I could achieve that only when out of uniform. I was even able to befriend a few locally based police officers who were gay. When I was with the other gay officers, I felt I could let my guard down and they'd look out for me. Most of the time we socialized at one of our homes since it was away from the public eye and a safer environment to be our true selves. None of us were truly out at work, but the others seemed more comfortable than I was, since they worked for an agency that was more accepting and less political. We'd drink and play cards, go out to gay bars on occasion, attend house parties, and watch movies. I was envious of their comfort in their identity and looked up to them. Sometimes Sampson would accompany me when I hung out with the gay officers but more often than not, he didn't since he didn't like the officer I'd gone to high school with.

I was slowly beginning to reconcile who I really was and contemplating how to bring myself out of the closet. It's one of the most challenging experiences of one's life. Everything your family and friends know about you, how they perceive you – everything is at stake. The reactions of loved ones could range from full acceptance to full abandonment. As Sampson and I dated, I refused to keep him a secret.

One of my brothers was set to get married and I wanted Sampson to attend the wedding—but not in a manner that would create a scene. I had a plan.

One afternoon, I paid a visit to Mom. We were close and could usually talk about anything. But this time I had a confession, and I was scared as to how she'd react. My dress rehearsal had been to tell my younger sister, Stacie, who accepted the news well. I told Mom I wanted to talk about who I was dating. We laughed a little about the topic and I felt a little more at ease.

But when I told her that I was dating a guy for several months, Mom began crying, which crushed me. I tried explaining the situation, but she was in a state of shock. She could only talk about the family I was giving up, clearly the only ideal future she had in mind for me. I told her I loved her and left. Mom had missed all of the hints I'd been dropping in the preceding months, like leaving out pronouns when I talk about dating or talking often about one of my gay cousins, and this was going to be a much longer process than I had imagined.

I eventually came out to my brothers and they didn't seem to care. One of them later converted to being a Jehovah's Witness and I met the news with the same acceptance that he had shown me. I told my old roommate Michelle of the news and she was supportive of me. She had her suspicions about my sexuality and wanted me to be happy, no matter who I loved.

Finally, I was coming out—and I beginning to gather support for being gay from those I cherished most. I knew how lucky I was; too many LGBTQ sons and daughters are disowned, which is infuriating and heartbreaking. My brother's wedding was approaching and would be held in November 2008, and he was supportive when I asked for Sampson to attend as my date. It would be held in Mom's backyard in King William County, VA. The only wild card was that my father and his wife were attending—and they were not aware of the news.

My father and I had been deepening our relationship somewhat, involving weekly phone calls to check in and visits when I was in Pennsylvania, mostly. My relationship with my stepmother was tepid at best. I couldn't figure her out and was worried about the influence she had on my father. Now I would be seeing my father and stepmother again on my own turf in Virginia. I wasn't sure how to handle the situation with Sampson. But I figured, fuck it; what's to lose?

On the day of my brother's wedding, I had already asked Mom and my brother for their permission and they both granted it, so I invited Sampson to come to Mom's house for the reception. I can't imagine how he felt walking into that nest of uncertainty, but he bravely did it. He met my mother, her husband, some family friends, and lastly, I introduced him to my father. Dad doesn't show emotion, so I'm not sure what he was thinking. But there wasn't any drama involved that night—and I was grateful for that.

A month later I was talking to Dad on the phone while on patrol. I called him every Sunday to catch up. In the background, I heard his wife yelling. She told him to inform me that Sampson was never welcome in their house. If I tried, she would have me arrested for trespassing. Dutifully, Dad repeated her ultimatum. I was absolutely crushed to be rejected by my own father; I broke down in tears and knew that our relationship had forever been changed. I wondered why he had resigned his spine to this woman. Why the relationship we'd spent so much time building would be callously tossed aside at the will of a third party. All I knew was that I wouldn't be returning to his home. Sampson was a part of my life; if they couldn't accept him, I took that as rejection of myself.

Mom and I agreed we wouldn't discuss my sexuality with my grandfather, Pap, as he was ninety years old. I idolized the man and wouldn't risk jeopardizing our relationship, though I knew deep down he wouldn't care, as he only wanted me to be happy. I took the same approach when it came to my paternal grandparents.

They were also nearing ninety and this wasn't something I felt they needed to know. They lived in western Pennsylvania so they would never meet Sampson. What I eventually learned is we don't give grandparents enough credit. They've lived through some intense times. They are way wiser than we think.

It felt great to have my family know the truth about who I was. But my relationship with Mom had now changed. There was awkwardness and gaps in conversation where they hadn't existed before. We'd always been close and able to freely talk about anything, but now a hesitation was present. I underestimated how long it would take her to process my sexuality and have a better understanding of it. It took about a year for her to come around and get back to the normalcy in our relationship, though it was still uncomfortable and painful at times. I had to slowly introduce Sampson into my regular conversations with her, so she could get more context as to how our relationship worked. The process developed slowly until we met for dinner at Mexico restaurant in Mechanicsville, so she could get to know Sampson. Once Mom saw how we interacted with each other and we were no different than any other couple, she began to let her guard down. She talked more freely and grew visibly more relaxed when Sampson was around. She saw how he interacted with my nieces and how much my sister liked him and warmed up to him herself. Mom was just one of many people who had never met a gay person before, and we were happy to educate everyone. We took pride in being out and proud, and showing people who we were as a couple and how we lived our lives, just like they did.

Things with Sampson were continuing to go well. But we had some growing pains. He was working for a local grocery chain as a store manager, but he was very unhappy; his degree was not in that field. I felt he should be happy, since he had a salary and benefits – at a time when the Richmond job market was suffering a recession.

One night, Sampson and I were out at a bar in Richmond. Out of the blue, my boyfriend suggested a three-way with some guy at the bar. I was completely caught off-guard by this. Tears began to flow and I had to leave the bar as fast as possible. I was crushed. I had always been in monogamous relationships; the thought of someone else in the relationship was appalling. I was forced to re-alize I had been fooling myself; things with Sampson weren't dan-dy at all.

We eventually discussed the matter, but the damage had been done. Sampson's suggestion created a damaging ripple that went far and wide in the relationship, deeper than I ever realized. We never discussed it again, and I told myself that he had no inten-tions of hurting me, as he's a gentle, loving, and sweet man. Things were uneasy going forward with Sampson, since on top of this is-sue I was dealing with the sudden disconnect from my father who I felt had betrayed me.

In the midst of this heartache, in April of 2009, I got news that Jeff, my close friend from high school and the Gus' family, was hos-pitalized. Jeff and I had been friends since middle school and were roommates twice in the years that followed. Jeff was a laid-back and jovial guy who never took himself seriously. We'd both worked at BB&T bank, both bought Nissan pickups around the same time, worked out together, and had an affinity for the beach and cars. We often took road trips together, socialized together, and our ex-panding friend circles overlapped a lot. We'd grown apart in recent years, but the news of his hospitalization was shocking. Jeff was in the emergency room with an organ rupture and sepsis. Before I knew it, he was dead at the age of 29.

The Sheriff's Office provided courtesy escorts for the local funeral homes. I requested the assignment, so I could have the honor of leading Jeff's procession from the funeral home to his final resting place. The Sheriff's Office didn't have a marked Mustang GT, or else I'd have used that, as Jeff was a Mustang enthusiast. On that sunny but sad afternoon, I led the most important funeral procession of my career.

Meanwhile, problems persisted with Sampson and I. For my part, I felt an internal angst building. One weekend, we went to the Outer Banks for a getaway, but the animosity was palpable. We were being curt with each other and since we were staying with friends of his and Doug, I went for lots of runs on my own to clear my mind. Things had been building up for me mentally and running was a way for me to process things. I think more clearly when I'm exercising and this was no different. Our sex life was lacking, and I felt like a backseat driver in my relationship, largely due to not standing up for myself and putting his needs and concerns above my own. I was always worried about what he would think or how he'd react to something. I was always walking on eggshells. This behavior may have been appropriate in the early stages of a relationship, but it had been well over a year for us, and the pattern was not healthy to either person. Though I'd been in prior relationships, I'd never actually been in love with someone. I was inexperienced when it came to the situation, but I knew this one didn't feel right.

Everything was coming to a head and we both sensed it. It began as a very tight-lipped drive back to Richmond, just the two of us for four hours on the interstate. We started the conversation two hours into the drive, trying to figure out what to do. Neither of us seemed happy. I didn't have many answers and when Sampson asked if I wanted to break up, I said yes. I didn't know what else to do or how to sort things out. I thought we needed a break from each other, to allow the tension to relax and look within for answers. After our difficult talk, we both fell silent for the remaining hour of the drive.

It didn't take long for Sampson to remove the few things he had at my place, again, but he still lived across the street with Doug, so it'd be difficult to avoid each other. I was saddened to lose him, as he was the only boyfriend I'd had and was my only exposure to the LGBTQ world. As with most changes in my life, I sold the Toyota Highlander I had owned and bought an Acura TSX right after Sampson and I split up. I felt freer to be myself and began reconnecting with friends I hadn't seen in a while, as well as spending more time with the gay officers group. We would hang out at Maymont or Bryan Park being sporty or along the James River if it was warm enough.

On the professional front, I was making progress on my attempts to get hired by a federal law enforcement agency. I had applied to the FBI and U.S. Secret Service in August of 2008. The hiring process was ungodly slow, but any progress was better than none at all. I wanted to make Pap proud and happy, so I kept him updated on my progress any time I went to Pennsylvania to spend time with him. There was nothing wrong with a career as a police officer. But I knew that I wanted to go the federal route. Due to my sexual orientation and the political nature of the Sheriff's Office, I surmised I could get promoted only to sergeant. I wanted the gold badge and salary that federal agents achieve, plus the new beginnings that would come by moving to a new state.

CHAPTER FIVE

IN SUMMER OF 2009, I WAS MAKING trips to D.C. to hang out with a guy. I met Justin during a drunken brunch following Obama's inauguration. While he was attractive, his stories of exaggerated grandeur were alarming. He claimed his father was a U.S. Attorney, as one example. He spent so much time creating falsehoods that he couldn't keep up with all of them. I should have been turned off, but we hung out anyway. I wasn't seeing anybody at the time and he served as a way to get to know the city and more people in D.C., where I hoped to live and work in the near future. We even took a road trip to Orlando. We got a bougie hotel in the city and explored the area together before driving back to DC, stopping in Jacksonville to hang out with friends of mine for a night. But once back in D.C. on a subsequent visit to Justin, I discovered a used condom just sitting on a shelf next to the bed, so that was the end of the line for us.

Shortly thereafter, D.C. Pride was looming. I'd never experienced one before, so I agreed to join one of the Richmond gay officers and his circle of friends for the festivities. We stayed at the Donovan Hotel on Thomas Circle, which was near the epicenter of D.C. Pride. It was mesmerizing to be surrounded by so many likeminded persons, comfortable in their own skin, unashamed of who they were. Attractive men abounded, and a lot of alcohol being consumed. I got goosebumps when I saw the Metropolitan Police Department actively participating in the Pride parade. It provided a glimmer of hope for me, that one day I'd be accepted for who I was while in uniform. I pondered the matter; if I didn't get hired as a federal agent, I could work for Metropolitan Police and request to work in the LGBTQ unit in Dupont Circle.

On the second night of the trip, we were crossing a street and I spotted Sampson and his ex-lover Doug. It certainly darkened my mood and probably explained why I drank a lot into the evening. After too many drinks, someone suggested going to the Crew Club, a gay bathhouse. Another first for me. I roamed around in a towel, curious. But as I explored the darker areas of the place, I was shocked by the sex I saw. I'd never seen group sex in person or some of the fetishes going on; I was very uncomfortable. This was not the place for me in my then-prudish ways, so I headed back to the hotel.

Pap was ninety-three at the time. For a few months Pap's organs had been slowing down. Congestive heart failure was setting in, as his lungs kept filling up with fluid. The doctors would drain them and then the cycle would repeat itself. I knew the time was close, as he told my Mom, who was looking after him, that he was tired and wanted to go "home." I made a visit to see him in May 2009, while he was still aware and able to communicate.

I got the call about my grandfather passing on July 1st and headed to D.C. I stayed at my ex-Justin's before connecting with my cousin Lisa. We had decided to drive together to Pennsylvania.

Her wife was traveling out of the country and I was single, so it made sense to be there for each other. In the middle of the night while at Justin's, I woke up crying loudly and hysterically. But my host never stirred, even though I needed someone's shoulder the most. I eventually went back to sleep. Justin never said a word. The next day, I headed out to meet my cousin, never to see or speak with Justin again. He ended up passing away a few years later, for reasons unbeknownst to me, back home in Indiana.

I wasn't super-close with Lisa at the time, but we were close enough to make small talk and endure the painful drive back home. We reserved a hotel in Indiana, Pennsylvania and joined the rituals surrounding funerals. I thought of Pap's legacy. He taught me a lot about life, morals, ethics, family life, giving back, and just being a good man. I hope to achieve the same standard, so that my grandkids could reflect on my legacy. Pap remains the most inspiring human I've ever met. Up until his nineties, he would visit the local elementary schools and give talks about his time in World War II.

The viewing at the funeral home was surreal, seeing Pap laid out in his comfortable clothes. I was talking with people who hadn't seen me since I was a kid. At the gravesite, I became more emotional. As he was laid next to grandma and they played taps, I lost control. Lisa pulled me into her shoulder. The finality of it was setting in. This was now the only place to visit my grandparents. I guess it was also the realization that life, like one layer of the onion, had been peeled away and now it was my parent's generation up next for mortality. I'd always had that protective layer and now it was gone, stripped away with the loss of the man who was my father figure and idol.

Pap was buried next to the love of his life on July 4, 2009. It was appropriate for him to be buried on Independence Day, since he was an all-American: An Army-Air Corps B-24 tail gunner, prisoner of war, retired U.S. Postal Courier, Hollywood bellhop (who met then-actor Ronald Reagan), ranch hand for Harry James and Betty Grable, farmer, adoptive parent, family man, hero. Pap left his money to the kids, the house to my mother, his farm to my uncle, and he left enough to buy his lady friend Stella a new car. I'll forever be grateful to have had this amazing man in my life as my moral compass for as long as I did, and he shaped me in ways he may have never known. Years after his passing, Pap's positive effect on the family reverberates still.

After his death, I settled into the grieving process for the first time. I took a trip to Pennsylvania and went to the old house. As I entered, a million memories flooded my mind. I slowly made my way through the house, touching the walls, seeing if he was there in spirit. It was hard but it felt like the right thing to do. I knew it'd be the last time I'd be at the house for a long time. I finally and reluctantly locked up and headed back for the graveyard to say a few words.

My grandfather appeared in my dreams for years. At first, it was frightening to see him again. Was he checking in on me? Eventually, I grew thankful to see him again. He appeared in a powerful dream eight years after he died, this time with my grandmother by his side. They were standing side by side in the living room of his house. I took a lot of comfort in that particular dream. They were reassuring me they were happily back together. It was at that moment that I knew I had finally processed the loss.

For some time, I had been experiencing a recurring pain in my abdomen. The symptoms would arrive early in the day, then worsen. I had been dealing with this for almost two years. The pain would cause me to throw up anything in my stomach. The pain sometimes forced to leave work early. By the time bedtime rolled around, I was usually in the fetal position and I'd simply endure the pain for the rest of the night. By the next morning it would begin to subside and take a day or so to fully go away.

I had paid visits to my physician and a gastroenterologist before, during, and after these episodes. But it was usually diagnosed as heartburn or something similar, despite having no triggering foods identified. This went on for two years. One night, I went to dinner at Texas Roadhouse with a work colleague who was aware of my recurring symptoms. When I refused to order anything, explaining that I'd only throw it up later, she insisted that I go to the ER to figure out the problem. No—she harangued me. So we went together.

I gave the attending physician my history. She did a CT scan and came back into the hospital room smiling and shaking her head. My appendix was currently inflamed. That made sense, as my brother's had ruptured a few years prior. She recommended it be removed as soon as possible, to prevent it from rupturing. I was relieved to have the problem identified and I wanted it out of my body immediately. I went into surgery a couple of hours later. The only problem post-surgery? Superficially worrying how the laparoscopic scars would affect my prized six-pack of ab muscles.

Sampson and I hadn't spoken for many months, but I received a text from him while I was in the hospital recovering from the appendix surgery, asking how I was. My sister, who worked as a banker in Ashland, Virginia, ran into Sampson in a local grocery store which he managed. She told him what had happened. I have to be honest; the summer had been pretty awful without him.

Once I was out of the hospital, Sampson and I met at his place, across the street from mine, to catch up. My stomach was in knots, not knowing where things would lead between us. Rather, he did some yardwork while we talked. There was a lot of ambivalence and angst on my end, but I wanted to reconcile things with him. In hindsight, I had only spent two months without him, so I hadn't had much time to experience being on my own. In my overly rational mind, I had determined that I needed Sampson, because I had learned so much from him, I had genuine feelings for him, and he was my sole connection to the gay world. He told me that he was very uncertain about going forward, based on our two previous break ups, but we were both willing to give it another shot.

I knew I was progressing in the hiring processes for the FBI and Secret Service, since background interviews had been conducted with family, neighbors, employers, and Sampson. I was scheduled for a polygraph examination. It took six hours and was one of the worst experiences I had ever had. I had been an upstanding airman and police officer, with a clean record and zero drug usage. But the interrogation left me feeling like a total dirt bag. A home visit was done by the Secret Service. They explained to me the specifics of the job, and all the benefits and drawbacks. My condo was always spotless and lacked any obvious sign that was I was gay, though I made no attempt to hide it. I just didn't offer a lot of information and it wasn't until late in the process that my background investigator realized Sampson and I were an item. Once the home visit was done, I was pretty close to getting an offer of employment. I asked the Sheriff's Office to move me to a calmer part of the county, where there were lower chances to make a lot of arrests that required court appearances, so I'd be free in case I got the call from the Feds.

Sampson was also aware of how quickly things were moving along. That made us both uncomfortable about where we stood in the relationship. One morning we were lying in bed, talking about the future. If I got the job, I didn't know where they would assign me – or how long I'd be gone for. That's when I floated the idea of solidifying things and getting married. I felt it was incumbent upon me to provide Sampson with some security. We agreed it was something to consider. At the time, it wasn't legal nationwide and was only legal in a handful of states, including Washington, DC.

Sampson had a ring from another suitor he'd received a couple of years prior. We took it to Jared Jewelers to trade in towards two platinum wedding bands, with eight diamonds across the top. We decided to get married in Boston, despite neither of us being there before. Out of the states where gay marriage was legal, it was a place we both wanted to visit. We booked flights to Boston for late October 2009, the day after I turned thirty.

We checked in at a gay-owned bed and breakfast in the middle of the city. Afterward, we headed to city hall to fill out the marriage application that required a waiting period. We meandered around Boston for a few days, taking in the sights, and pinpointing the ideal wedding location – despite having no wedding permit. Since it was close to Halloween, we took the train to Salem to see where the "witches" were hung. The temperatures were a tad cooler than expected, but it was a great time to explore the Boston area.

Admittedly, I was nervous to get married, as I had witnessed

Mom go through multiple husbands and I worried I would make the same mistakes. Though Sampson and I had discussed the issues we encountered in the past, I still didn't fully allow my true self to show to him, much to my own detriment. I wanted this man in my life and I planned to do whatever it would take to make it happen – even squelching my true personality.

A day prior to the wedding, Doug and my best friend from the Sheriff's Office arrived. We were the first gay couple we knew of to get married. For the wedding day, we had decided on wearing black suits. We decided it would be easier to flee into the park and blend in with the crowd if the wedding permit police showed up. The justice of the peace we had hired online was just as giddy and delightful as we had hoped. We all walked to Boston Public Garden, next to the pond, to make it official. In the mid-morning of October 29th, we exchanged our vows in front of the massive audience of three. My vows were on a sheet of paper and Sampson's was on his iPhone.

We exchanged rings—and it was all over before we knew it. It wasn't at all what I had imagined as my wedding day, missing our families and friends, in a strange city. While I was externally happy, I felt as though I should've been more ecstatic. Maybe we were missing the fanfare that accompanies weddings. Our marriage was barely legal. And my thoughts were distracted by memories of our multiple breakups and my looming career change. We went to Houston's restaurant, where Doug paid for the entire lunch. Then it was time to trek back to Richmond.

Back home, we continued to live apart, since a job move for me was likely to happen in the near future. But Sampson said he would move with me wherever I was assigned. Our families were generally supportive about the wedding news. Our friends were lukewarm about it. At the Sheriff's Office, I didn't mention the wedding to anyone. Most didn't even notice the wedding ring on my left hand, as straight men are generally oblivious to things like that. I was working the central part of the county, which allowed me to respond to critical things in the east and west side of the county. But my area, Hanover Airpark, was generally quiet after hours.

In early December 2009, Sampson and I were heading to the gym one morning in Short Pump. My phone rang. It was the Special Agent in Charge (SAIC) of the U.S. Secret Service, Richmond Field Office. I was both apprehensive and excited that "the call" finally arrived. The Agent in Charge asked if I was still interested in a position with the Secret Service and I calmly said yes. He said I would have to accept the position with a hire date of January 3, 2010 and select from one of the six locations available. I grabbed a dry-cleaning slip I had in the car and hurriedly wrote down the locations he listed. Sampson sat nervously next to me, for his life was also being flipped upside down at that moment. The boss said I had a day or two to think about the location I would prefer, and to call him back once I had made our decision.

There we sat in the parking lot of American Family Fitness. I was holding a small pink dry-cleaning slip with the following field office locations scribbled on it: Los Angeles, New York, Miami, Newark, New Jersey, Albany, New York, and Jackson, Mississippi. We were both thrilled to have the news we'd waited so long for. But Washington, D.C., the location we desired, wasn't even mentioned. We went into the gym for a distracted workout and then rushed home to figure out our futures.

We quickly googled the cost of living, rent prices, distance, and job markets of all the candidate cities, since I had to report to the Sheriff's Office for my afternoon shift. Sampson would be moving without a job and my pay varied, based off of the cost of living in the respective city. We would be a single-income household until Sampson found work. The Secret Service didn't pay for the initial move/relocation expenses, so we had to factor that into the decision. Based on my hiring salary, we knew we couldn't afford New York City or Los Angeles. Neither of us wanted to move to Newark, and the thought of living in Mississippi as a married gay couple terrified us.

I went into the Sheriff's Office for roll call and broke the news to my Sergeant that I would be submitting my two-weeks' notice. This was December 10, 2009 and my final day of patrol would be December 24, 2009. I decided to take a week off for the holidays, to prepare myself, pack, and visit family before training in early January. We were in the middle of roll call when I was summoned to take a phone call in an adjacent room. It was the Special Agent in Charge, asking what my choice of field office was. I told him Miami.

It was bittersweet to give notice. The agency I had matured with, my peers I'd depended on to have my back, the unbreakable bonds would be difficult to replace. I didn't know how things would shape up at the federal level, but it was a risk I was willing to take. Mom wasn't exactly thrilled that I would be moving a thousand miles away, but she was supportive. I would be leaving in early January for the Federal Law Enforcement Training Center in Gylnco, Georgia, for four months to complete the Criminal Investigator Training Program. Sampson would remain back in Richmond until my training was complete. In the short window before I was to leave for Georgia, I also had to sell my condo. The country was at the onset of the economic meltdown and home prices were plummeting fast. I wasn't sure how I was going to overcome the loss on the condo while paying realtor fees and relocation expenses for both Sampson and me. But it had to be done in order to make the move to Miami feasible.

Around that same time, I came to the conclusion that though my father had told me my husband wasn't ever welcomed in his home without the police being called, he was still my father and the only one that I had. I didn't want to continue to avoid him and one day get a phone call that he passed from a heart attack or something, and then have to live with regret. I resumed calling him sporadically to check in and talk, even visiting him when I was in town to see my grandparents in Pennsylvania. The pink elephant stood large in the room, as I weighed starting a dramatic fight with his wife versus the odds that she would win and further isolate him from his grown son. In my mind, that was her goal, and I wouldn't allow her to achieve it, so Dad and I avoided discussing that conversation and the hurt it caused. I swallowed my pride, put the hurt aside, and resumed normal contact with my father. I would curtail my visits to ensure Sampson would never be put in an uncomfortable position or be seen as anything less than my equal. One weekend while visiting Richmond for a Jehovah Witness convention, Dad brought all of his tools and we renovated the two bathrooms in my condo. It was his comfort zone, his mastery, and it was a great time to reconnect as father and son.

I hired a realtor and had been prepping the condo in anticipation of the job offer, so it was ready to market immediately. Dad and I had redone the bathrooms, the walls and kitchen cabinets repainted, and new blinds installed. In my community, it was the cleanest and most updated condo on the market.

December 24 rolled around, my final day on patrol. It was a slow evening in the center part of the county. I was thinking about news reports, TV and movie plots I had seen where police officers are shot the day before leaving the job or retirement, so I was all about hiding somewhere. The sergeant on duty told me to head home early, as my peers would handle any calls that came in. I was both excited and melancholy when I picked up the car radio microphone for the last time to contact dispatch. I told them unit 231 would be 10-42 (out of service), thanked them for their service, and told my peers to stay safe.

Just like that, my time as a patrol officer was done.

I walked away from the Sheriff's Office a wiser and matured individual. They provided me with a foundation for success that I still rely on to this day. I've kept in contact with some officers. When I pass through town now while visiting Mom, it's a flashback to see familiar faces on patrol and catch up. The men and women in uniform are angels among us.

On January 3, 2010, I reported for duty to the Richmond Field Office as a Special Agent Trainee (I hated that last part). For the previous six years, I had worn a badge on my uniform, had a good reputation within my agency, a defined role, a familiarity in what I was doing. But now I was relegated to a fucking new guy again. I spent two weeks helping with administrative tasks, helping relocate the office, and attending a two-day Special Agent introductory training course. I fully expected to be treated like a basic training recruit, subject to yelling and pushups—but, unexpectedly, I was treated like an adult.

I met my classmates, with whom I would be spending the next nine months, and our class coordinators. We spent two days in the D.C. area, were issued our Blackberry phones (which made me feel special and important, despite being neither). We received our code of conduct and a general overview of the coming months. After two days in Maryland, we reported to the Federal Law Enforcement Training Center (FLETC) in Georgia to get certified as a criminal investigator. The course included firearms, control tactics, physical fitness and lots of classroom time. The federal training center standard for passing tests was seventy percent, but the Secret Service demanded we score a minimum of eighty percent on all tests. Fail a test and you're out of the program. I gave myself a pep talk, insisting there was zero chance I was going to mess up, since so much was at stake.

I drove my car from Richmond to Georgia so I wouldn't be confined to the training center campus. I looked forward to road trips on weekends to visit friends in Jacksonville or family in Savannah. On our first day, we learned our training class would be comprised of half IRS Criminal Investigators and half Secret Service agents. The IRS agents were wicked smart, but none of them came from a law enforcement background, as most of us were former police officers and military. The Secret Service recruits were in great physical shape, accustomed to the paramilitary environment, and spending most of our off time in the gym or studying.

I studied a lot while at the training center, as I wanted to make it through the course – rather than return to the Sheriff's Office with my tail between my legs. I rewrote the notes from the lectures and turned them into study guides that many classmates borrowed. It annoyed me at first, but I developed a sense of teamwork and wanted everyone to succeed. Our class of twenty-three was becoming tight knit. I befriended the old man of the group, Jim. He was also from the Pittsburgh area, a former Marine, strong as an ox, and a jovial guy. Although he smoked like a freight train, he was fun to hang around and provided a place to let my guard down. Jim drove a Ford F-150 with a large purple stripe down the side, so it was appropriate that he was the first person I told I was gay. I felt comfortable around him, since he was mature, and we had similar personalities.

My husband Sampson and I had planned to spent Valentine's day together, since it fell during a three-day weekend which would allow me to drive back to Richmond. But Mother Nature had other plans. A winter storm was threatening to drop a lot of snow in an area that never gets snow. I can drive in snow, but I'd argue most Southerners cannot. The further north I drove on 95, the worse the snow got. At one point, I-95 was a one-lane road and I was stuck in my little Acura TSX behind a tractor-trailer doing about twenty-five miles per hour and dropping snow chunks on my hood. I decided to end the drive just north of Savannah before things got any worse. I called Sampson and we concocted a plan to fly him to Savannah the next morning and we'd just spend the weekend there. We stayed in a hotel near the waterfront and explored the city. It was the reprieve we both needed, he from the rigors of managing grocery stores and mine from my training. It was the first trip we'd had since our wedding. We ate at Paula Deen's restaurant, got tipsy on boozy slushies, walked the beach on Tybee Island, and enjoyed the St. Patrick's Day celebrations.

In March 2010, I accepted an offer on my condo in Richmond. It was less than I hoped, but the market was worsening, so I accepted it. The closing was set for April. The only issue was I needed to bring a check for $25,000 to closing since the value had been steadily dropping. I surely didn't have that money sitting around, but this deal had to happen, in order for me to move to Miami after training. I called my mother for a loan. It was a tough thing to do, as I'm very independent. She bailed me out and the condo went to closing. I later cashed out my retirement with the county and got a whopping $13,000, which I immediately gave to Mom.

Things at the federal training center were going well and the months flew by. Two superstars spoke to our class one afternoon. Jerry Parr was the USSS Special Agent who saved Ronald Reagan's life in 1981 during the Hinckley assassination attempt. Clint Hill had been in Dallas that fateful November day in 1963. He jumped on the back of the presidential limo and shielded Jackie Kennedy. The weight of what these two men had witnessed was evident in their speeches. The class hung on every word they said.

In late April, we made it to graduation, with twenty-three of us intact. I received the academic award, the driving award, and shooting award. I missed the physical fitness award since I'm as flexible as a piece of lumber. I now had the status of a criminal investigator in the government ranks. If I were to fail out of the Secret Service specific portion of the training, I could potentially be employed elsewhere as an agent. I felt more confident as we began the transition to Maryland for a few more months of training. Our class had a week-long break between training academies. Neither Sampson nor I had ever been to Miami. My assigned location and hadn't a clue what to expect. I had been contacting property managers in downtown Miami to assist us in finding a condo to rent. We had a few options lined up.

We headed to the land of sunshine to spend a few days. Sampson's roommate Doug came along on the trip, as he was familiar with Miami on his multiple prior visits and helped absorb some of the costs involved. Despite my reservations, he turned out to great company, as he was a seasoned traveler and a foodie. We explored the Brickell neighborhood, where condo towers crowded the skyline. We went to Met1 to see a new two-bedroom condo on the thirty-fourth floor. The condo was brand-new, floor-to-ceiling windows overlooking the Miami River, Biscayne Bay, and partial views of the ocean. We were in awe of the place, even with its higher price tag. We signed a lease and spent the rest of the trip on South Beach relaxing.

Since I was considered out of district from the Washington, D.C. area, the Secret Service put me and my classmates in an extended-stay hotel with a decent per diem allowance. We had clunky vans for commuting to and from the training center, a routine for the next four months. Sampson came to visit a couple of weekends and I would head back to Richmond for visits on weekends. The training wasn't easy but at no time did I feel like I wouldn't make it through the academy. The academic portion came a little easier, as I had my study habits down and we had study sessions at the hotel. I was taught everything there is to know about counterfeit U.S. currency, since the Secret Service was originally founded to protect United States currency. We were also trained in white collar financial crimes, and protection—the most common role of Secret Service agents. A few weeks in, a classmate couldn't pass an exam and was booted out. It was alarming to see a peer thrown out of the program but also a reminder they only wanted the best agents and didn't bend the rules for anybody.

We'd have physical training sessions four to five days a week and it coincided with the rise in popularity of CrossFit. CrossFit was the crux of our fitness program. As a class of type-A personalities, we were constantly competing with each other. There was a control tactics portion followed up with our fitness training, so we'd often work out for two hours or more per day. I sustained myself on tuna packets and the caveman/paleo diet of fruits, vegetables, and nuts. I could tell I was losing weight, but there really wasn't much weight to lose. My body fat was soon below five percent! I was the fastest person in my class and ran a nineteen-minute three-mile run, adding my name to the list on the wall at the academy, where it still remains to this day. I was feeling more confident in my appearance, with great abs, veins showing in places they hadn't before, and knowing I could handle myself on the street. However, I was cautious to not appear cocky or vain.

Finally, the end of August arrived, and we twenty-two Special Agent Trainees graduated from the academy. We were excited to be sent into the field where the real work would commence. Photos were taken in front of the flags and USSS emblem with Mom and Sampson. I'd wished Pap had lived to see the ceremony. We were presented with our credentials, weapons, badges, and other goodies. We were officially Special Agents and it felt good to carry a badge again, but this time a gold-colored one. Three of our graduates were sent to the Miami Field Office, with the others scattered across the country.

After leaving the ceremony, there was a congratulatory luncheon for me at my cousin Lisa's house in Arlington. It was a bittersweet occasion, as I was actually moving away from home for Miami. And Sampson was moving without any job awaiting him. Mom presented me with a card that announced that she had forgiven the remaining eight thousand dollars of debt as my graduation present. Lisa gave me the revolver once owned by my grandfather. When he died a year prior, we found it in the arm of his recliner—the same recliner where his grandkids and great-grandkids had played for years.

As the meal ended, it was time for goodbyes. My mother usually wasn't very emotional. But as she hugged me, she burst into tears and ran out of the house. It was a touching moment.

We rented a mid-sized Budget rental truck and a trailer for the car. We didn't trust U-Haul, as I would always see their broken-down trucks along the highway. We had to fit both of our belongings into this truck, in addition to our newly adopted Bengal cat Leslie and Jack Russell Terrier Baxter. We had a thousand-mile drive ahead of us. The next morning, we loaded the newer Acura TSX that we had traded both of our cars in for, onto the trailer and began the trek south. Sampson was wrought with emotion as he hugged his former lover, best friend, confidant, and roommate Doug goodbye. I felt badly for him, knowing he was taking a large gamble on me and our future, but I was also a little relieved. I wouldn't have to compare myself to Doug and could focus on building Sampson and I's identity as a married couple. I assured Sampson it would all be okay, though only time would help ease the pain.

We would take I-95 the entire way to Miami but planned to stop in Jacksonville for a night to stay with friends. Driving was uneventful, but it seemed like we stopped every few hours to fill up. I estimated it cost several hundred dollars in gas to get to Florida. The pets were in the cab with us and bored out of their minds, but the trip went seamlessly. The song "House That Built Me" by Miranda Lambert kept coming on the radio on our drive and was the perfect song for our move.

CHAPTER SIX

WE ARRIVED IN MIAMI SAFELY. But we couldn't access the loading dock at the condo for unloading until the next morning. We emptied the car and found a local Budget rental facility in Calle Ocho, where we could drop the car trailer. We were a day early in returning the car trailer, and the guy demanded to be paid cash for allowing us to return it early. I found an ATM so I could pay the jackass. This was my initiation into Miami culture. We returned the car trailer and found a spot to park the moving truck until the next morning when we could unload it. Our new home was at the corner of Biscayne Boulevard and Route 1, adjacent to the Intercontinental Hotel and down the street from American Airlines Arena.

One of my squad mates picked me up for my first day in the Miami Field Office. He was a man of deep voice but few words, which was intimidating. But I eventually realized he was a friendly guy. Our government-issued vehicles had been pre-selected for us. Mine was a beat-up Impala that I named Goldie. She would sometimes conk out while driving, but I was happy to have a take-home government ride.

I was assigned to the counterfeit squad. I soon realized some people in the office already knew that I was gay. I was both surprised and alarmed by this. I couldn't figure out how people in Miami already knew. I didn't want my sexuality to be how fellow agents referred to me, but the secret was out before I stepped foot into the office. Within the first week, I was approached by a counterfeit technician who introduced himself. He was friendly, bubbly, and more flamboyant than I was but he was happy to have someone else on team gay. Instead of embracing his kinship, I kept things professional for fear of how it may impact my reputation and probably a dose of self-loathing in there as well. I wasn't aware of any other gay agents in the office. I was doing all I could to conceal my sexuality until I knew who I could trust and if being out would negatively affect my career. I was still on probation and could be fired for any reason.

One female agent in my squad knew that I was gay and reached out to an Assistant U.S. Attorney who was also gay to connect us. I was appreciative that she wanted to introduce me, but not happy she was outing me to complete strangers. In the straight male-dominated world of law enforcement, releasing such information must be done in a strategic manner. I pulled the agent aside and explained my discomfort and annoyance to her, explaining that this wasn't something to be cavalier about and is a decision that only I can make. During our conversation, she apologized for outing me to the U.S. Attorney. Shortly thereafter, a senior agent, who was a lesbian, informed me the Special Agent in Charge had told her in advance that I was coming to the office. So I realized my sexual orientation was an open secret from the top down all along.

This was my first lesson in learning that there are no secrets in the Secret Service. I had played it coy during the academy and was not carrying a Rainbow Flag around, as some of my classmates didn't even know I was married to a man. I wasn't embarrassed by it, but fearful of how those in positions of power may react to it. I was in the gym with the rest of the guys most mornings and even participated in the "keg challenge" to show the Special Agent in Charge that I could physically hold my own. I didn't want to be defined by my sexuality and the misconceptions that gay men were anything less than heterosexual men. Admittedly, I had bought into the idea that effeminate gay men were less acceptable than masculine gays.

Since Sampson was seeking employment and had managerial experience in retail, I asked the agent who handled liaising with area hotels if he had any job contacts. But he was the only one who I had hinted to that I was gay. I later discovered that the agent who outed me to the U.S. Attorney was friends with the lesbian agent and they often had lunch with the agent who handled the hotel contacts. When I learned the agent was also outing another closeted agent in the office, our relationship soured.

In February 2011, I was reassigned to the Miami Multi-Agency Task Force aka the Airport Squad. I would now be assigned to the Miami and Fort Lauderdale International Airports (and any other airport in South Florida), handling all protective visits, mail intercepts, and other duties. This transfer struck me as very odd. I was now working with two very senior agents and a supervisor, all eligible for retirement. My two classmates remained in the main field office, working in criminal squads, but I had been exiled.

I didn't want to make waves, so I worked hard to make a name for myself. It was a lot to learn at first, but I watched my colleagues. Both had been in the service for over twenty years. One was nicknamed "the Mayor of Miami." His entire career had been in the Miami Field Office district, so he was well-connected. While these veterans knew their stuff, they were no longer proactive. We'd get foreign heads of state to and from their planes and have café con leche with the Miami-Dade cops. I can't estimate the miles I walked around the Miami International Airport on duty.

I had my first federal arrest when a guy flew in from South America with $250,000 of counterfeit U.S. currency sewn into his pants. He was a mule, paid a small amount to smuggle. I wasn't thrilled about being stuck at a desk in the Field Office, buried in thousands of documents to prove bank fraud, mortgage fraud, or credit card fraud, so this was fine by me. Counterfeit arrests at the street level aren't as sexy to an Assistant U.S. Attorney as larger fraud loss cases, but I felt my work had more of an impact.

I assisted one of the senior agents when then-President Obama made a visit to Miami in the spring of 2011. It was eye-opening to say the least. I had never seen so many different tasks operating at the same time and come together simultaneously to ensure the President would be safe. The number of meetings I had to attend, the amount of paperwork involved, the endless emails, phone calls—and, worst of all, the stress involved. You wanted to ensure your supervisors were happy and the supervisors of the President's detail, on top of a no-fail mission. There is no room for error and the pressure is omnipresent. If the President were to get hurt while at your location or something to go awry that grabs the media's attention, it is your name and the name of the agent from the President's detail that'll forever be known.

A few months later, I found myself as the agent from the field office who would represent the Miami Office and handle a presidential visit to Miami. I would be the agent responsible for liaising with all of the Miami entities involved, guaranteeing we were all on the same page, and assisting with developing a plan to ensure it went seamlessly. It was a fantastic experience.

When Air Force One and POTUS arrive, we need to close down the entire airport. That's a big deal for the airspace in a city like Miami. The number of agencies involved in the operation was mind-boggling, but it ran like a well-oiled machine. The Miami-Dade police had done countless POTUS visits and I trusted their judgement.

But once the Presidential Protective Division (PPD) airport agent got into district, that's when things soured. He was my first PPD counterpart interaction. The guy thought he was God's gift to the world. He was cocky, arrogant, and rude to everyone: me, the other agents, and the Miami-Dade Police. That unexpected annoyance came on top of an incoming Miami summer thunderstorm.

Since I was the airport agent for that visit, I was able to get Sampson and a friend onto the airport grounds. Just prior to Obama's arrival, a storm rolled over the airport and completely drenched me. Afterward, my radio no longer worked, and I was having to relay information via cell phone. When Obama came off of Air Force One and walked over to greet the viewing public, Sampson and our friend both got to shake his hand. I stood off to the side in a wet black suit that was now steaming in the hot south Florida sun.

I absolutely loved living on the water in downtown Miami. I joined the Brickell Running Club. It was a great way to meet people and explore the area. The scenery was always amazing, and the water provided a calming effect for this Scorpio. I would go for runs along the waterfront, down through Brickell to Biscayne Bay and back north to Bayside Park. The homeless population tended to coalesce in that area—but who could blame them with the scenery and tourism dollars. There were legitimate mega-yachts that would dock right in front of our building. I would google the yacht name so I could learn the dimensions, year built, sale prices, and sometimes the owner. The people of Miami wholly believe in conspicuous consumption and it was on full display. The ultra-high-end cars, anything from Porsches to Bentleys to Rolls-Royces, were always in sight. There was even a Bugatti Veyron driving around South Beach. But after a few months of living there, the wow factor wore off and I wouldn't even turn my head to see an obnoxious tourist in a rented a Ferrari, driving like an asshole.

After a stressful month of searching, Sampson found work at CB2, a store owned by Crate and Barrel, on South Beach. Living in downtown Miami in 2010 had its perks, but also its negatives. For Sampson, the downside was dealing with traffic to and from the beach daily. The only place walkable for entertainment then was Mary Brickell Village—and there wasn't a lot. We cooked at home most nights, as my salary the first year wasn't very high. Thankfully, we had saved prudently while I was in training status.

We found ourselves spending lots of time socializing in South Beach, a very gay area with upscale stores, restaurants and wild gay bars and clubs. On one occasion, we'd had a night out at the bars, hitting Mova, Score, and Twist. We walked out of Twist, the sun was up, and we were too drunk to try and drive home, so we slept in the back of the TSX. It wasn't exactly comfortable for me, over six feet tall, but it was way better than a jail cell.

Sampson grew to detest commuting to and from SoBe. So as our first year in Miami drew to a close, we started looking at places in South Beach.

We were thoroughly enjoying the attractions SoBe had to offer, including the eye candy. One night at Twist in December 2010, we were dancing with another couple, a slender Columbian guy with a coy smile and his partner, a fit Mexican American guy. Unexpectedly, some heavy petting suddenly developed between the four of us while dancing. For someone who had priggishly insisted on monogamy, this was quite a change of scene. Either it was the booze or I was finally ready to bend a little. Everyone was making out with each other and having a great time.

Sampson and I soon left the bar in search of food and went next door to the BK Whopper Bar, where we ran into the couple again. We exchanged phone numbers with them. They had been together about as long as Sampson and I had, and they lived nearby in North Miami Beach. I hadn't been in the situation before, where I was making out with someone and my husband was doing the same, but it added a layer of excitement – especially where our sex life had been lacking for some time. Sampson and I talked about the boys and discussed how we felt about what had happened. Neither of us was hurt or seemingly jealous. We were both relieved. We made a pact that as long as we check in with each other's feelings about such situations, there was no harm done. We didn't have a plan to make it a regular thing or seek out similar opportunities but didn't rule it out, either.

A couple of weeks later we met up with the same boys again for cocktails and dancing. We danced and made out with each other for a couple of hours. I was having a great time and a couple of drinks had squelched my inhibitions and prudishness. When the boys invited us back to their house, Sampson and I were at a crossroads; we checked in with each other to see how each felt about the situation. He was agreeable from the start. I told Sampson I was okay and we agreed to go back to their place. We didn't discuss ground rules per se but would check in with each other as needed.

We got a tour of their home and chatted a bit before the making out recommenced with us swapping partners. Clothes began to come off as we were led to their bedroom, where they (thankfully) had a king-sized bed. We fell into the bed and I was focused on the Columbian lad while Sampson was manhandling the Mexican American lad. I didn't feel comfortable enough to have intercourse; I considered it a much more personal adventure and I wasn't mentally prepared to witness my husband engaging in it with another man – nor for him to see me plowing another man. But we did everything else. Once the four of us had satisfied our animalistic instincts, we attempted to sleep. We were sandwiched together in the one bed, where it felt like a cucumber was poking my back the rest of the night.

The next day, after we got back home, Sampson and I talked at length about the boys and the prior night. He was relieved that my attitude had changed and I was more open to adventures. I was certain to ensure I was okay with everything. It felt great to do something risqué and also see Sampson enjoy himself as well. We had never synced very well sexually and maybe this was a way to overcome that obstacle, as long as we remained together when doing so. We agreed we'd keep in contact with the boys and develop those relationships, since we didn't have many friends and they were a fun couple.

Two months later, on another night out to the bars, we met a Puerto Rican guy in his early twenties, with beautiful long eyelashes and a smile that lit up the room. He was into Sampson and I. We shared a cab back to our condo. Sampson and I had not had company in our own bed before, so this was a first for us. We agreed there wouldn't be any intercourse and, in the morning, the beaux had to go. After showering the smoke from the club off, we had another challenge: what to do with this man's massive penis. We both rose nobly to the occasion, then showered again and went to sleep. The next morning, we sent him on his way and checked in with each other again. We realized that we had to establish some ground rules for how this was going to work. What to do in the possible scenario where a guy will only be into one of us? We agreed to keep the focus on each other's feelings and not allow someone to come between us. If any difficult situations arose, we would maintain open communication between us and address the problem.

While driving back and forth to SoBe for work, Sampson had come across a newly renovated apartment community, at Alton and 20th Street next to the golf course, so we went to check it out. The one-bedroom apartment was several hundred dollars cheaper than the downtown condo we had, was walkable to everything including Publix and the gay bars, and a few blocks from Sampson's work on Lincoln Road. This meant we could sell the Acura and save money on car insurance and a car payment. In August 2011, we moved to South Beach. We hired guys to move us, but they were two twinky Eastern European guys who couldn't carry the weight. I had a broken arm in a cast from a rollerblading accident but had to help the movers. What a nightmare!

The apartment was 600 square feet with only one bedroom and

a galley kitchen, so it was snug for two men with a cat and a dog. But it was brand-new, overlooking the pool and golf course, and within stumbling distance to the bars.

I didn't see it at the time but Sampson and I had a new routine: we were spending more and more time at the bars. It was a way to lower my inhibitions and I had a good tolerance for drinking, usually vodka cranberry's. Boozing was a way to meet new people. Now there was the added perk of potentially finding someone to bring home with us. The bar hopping was confined to the weekends and at no time did it affect either of our jobs. We were new to Miami and assumed this was how it was supposed to be. Sampson and I were enabling each other to some degree and I was the newly created "good time Charlie," wanting the good times to continue. Sampson was better at monitoring things than I was, even though it was harder for me to hear it.

Eventually my year in the airport squad passed. A supervisor lobbied on my behalf and I was sent to the counterfeit squad, which was actually where I wanted to go. Among the fifteen fellow agents, I had a blast. While in the squad, I noticed a pattern of decent counterfeit $100 bills floating around the area, from Miami to West Palm Beach County. I decided to figure out the source, since the fraud loss was getting high in our area. I did not expect that this case would take up end up most of my time for the next two years.

The investigation had me driving from Miami to West Palm Beach regularly and I often enlisted my peers, who were always willing to help. Most of us lived in Broward County and it was easy to jump on Interstate 95 and get to Delray Beach or Pompano Beach in the middle of the night if there was something suspicious afoot. For instance, an arrest by a county officer and an interview would be needed. The local officers were making multiple arrests of people who possessed and used counterfeit currency, and each arrest could provide information that was previously unknown. In order to get closer to the source, I had to find out where the people were getting it from and work my way up the chain.

I began to compile large amounts of information and revealed an expansive network people passing the counterfeit, with three potential sources where they were buying it from. It was gratifying to put the pieces of the puzzle together. Jumping into the work car and meeting up with peers on a weekend or weeknight was commonplace since the bad guys usually aren't working bankers' hours. But my colleagues never complained. This was the life I envisioned being a federal agent and I loved it. As long as we were working cases and making arrests, our boss allowed us full autonomy. But if we were in the weeds, he would be by our sides at a moment's notice. He'd be a part of the team; he would roll out with us, do surveillances, process evidence, and make arrests. We all thrived in that squad thanks to his great leadership. He was the type of supervisor I hoped to be one day.

Living on South Beach was fun. We'd begun making friends and would meet up on the beach on weekends or host small gatherings. A guy we had met living in downtown Miami had also moved to South Beach, so boozing on the "gay" beach with him and others became a thing. We enjoyed doing happy hours and we would rotate hosting at everyone's homes. But once you live in a resort town, you soon take it for granted. We rarely went to the beach after a few months, quickly falling into the daily grind. We sold the Acura shortly after moving and Sampson coveted a scooter to get around the beach, since he had one in college. I had learned to ride one during a recent business trip to Honolulu and I loved it. Sampson and I went to the Vespa dealer on SoBe and test-drove an LX50. It rode like a dream. As Christmas 2011 approached, I secretly went back to the Vespa dealer and ordered a red LX50 with a tan saddle. I surprised my husband by bringing it to work, wrapped in a large bow. When he saw it, Sampson's jaw dropped and tears ran down his face. That moment was priceless.

We named the Vespa Gloria, a feisty Latina, and we rode her all over creation. Though it was only 50cc, it would do 45mph with both of us on it. One time, we rode her as far north as Aventura Mall, fifteen miles each way, where I once bought too many shoes, making it an awkward ride home. Sampson's mood changed when he was on Gloria. He lit up like a kid on Christmas morning, whether driving or riding, it didn't matter. It was a happy place for him and I loved to see him grinning in the side mirrors.

While working on SoBe, Sampson had met an attractive guy I will call Tom, just before the Vespa Christmas of 2011. Tom was mutual friends with the couple from North Miami Beach we had befriended and played with. Sampson invited me to meet Tom and his friends at Score one night and I gleefully went along. Tom was half Filipino and half German; with a confidence and directness I'd not seen before in a gay man. He was sassy and had a rapid-fire wit. I warmed to him rapidly.

Tom and his friends were fun, laid-back, and genuine—something that I found to be rare in Miami and SoBe. I had gone out of my way to try and make friends, inviting neighbors for social hours, etc. and I was met with curt and cold responses. I assumed they thought I wanted something from them, but I was only being neighborly. Tom and his friends lived in Fort Lauderdale and invited us to join them on their annual Christmas light boat tour. In Fort Lauderdale and Wilton Manors, residents have a tradition where they decorate their yards that line the waterways and canals, so the Christmas lights reflected off of the water. Boaters ride by at night to enjoy them. Not only was the boat tour beautiful, but these guys were a blast to be around. They drank as much as we did, they held great jobs, were modest, flirtatious, and many of them were attractive.

Tom was close friends with multiple other gay couples who had been together for years. It was reassuring to see other gay couples flourishing. We were invited to return the next night for a Christmas party at the home of another guy in their crowd. Though the host was a few years older than we were, he and his partner were friendly. They lived in a very nice section of Fort Lauderdale, Seven Isles, right on the intercoastal waterway. The booze flowed endlessly at the party. At one point, guests were running around the property wearing only bubble bath bubbles that had been poured into the hot tub, which then overflowed into the pool. I hadn't experienced such non-judgmental friends before and was happy to participate in the liberating shenanigans. I had come a long way in a short amount of time regarding my prudish views. The group was open, drama-free, and fun-loving. Sampson and I finally had found the friends we had been seeking since leaving Richmond.

We were invited regularly to hang out with the Fort Lauderdale crew on most weekends out by the pool, on a boat, or at a nearby resort. Alcohol was standard. All was good—until we had to face the drive back to Miami. That was the worst part since we were pretty buzzed and had to wait around to sober up.

The boys would often come to Miami Beach, so we would merry up with them. They liked that the infamous Palace drag bar, as well as Score, Mova, and Twist, were blocks from our apartment.

Tom was becoming a closer friend. We were hanging out more. He was the single one of the group. Sampson and I had hooked up with Tom a time or two, so the awkwardness was behind us. This didn't seem to present any problems between Sampson and I, nor the rest of the friends. Our open relationships provided a good foundation for friendship.

On one occasion, Tom and I went to Swinging Richards in North Miami Beach (male strip bar), as Sampson had to work the next morning. The drinks were strong. Thankfully, Tom was driving, because I was quite drunk. He decided to stop on the way home for McDonalds. When his order arrived, the smell of his food was nauseating; within minutes, I was throwing up into that same McDonalds bag. I felt awful about the situation, but Tom was easygoing and didn't give me a hard time.

As several months passed, we grew closer to the Fort Lauderdale boys and decided to move to that area. That would cease the weekend drives to and from Miami. We decided to find a house in Wilton Manors, for its proximity to the friends, high per capita of gays, and reasonable cost of living. This meant we would need to buy a car for Sampson to commute. He wanted a sensible Honda Civic.

Parking on Miami Beach was a nightmare. At times, I'd have to circle the block repeatedly until a spot opened up. Sampson had found a parking space for the new Civic he had purchased, adjacent to the Publix grocery store. But a Coke tractor trailer sideswiped the car and then left. The car had less than a thousand miles on it and was already involved in a hit-and-run. Welcome to Miami.

Our time on South Beach drew to a close in July 2012 but not before flying Mom down for her 55th birthday. She'd never been there, and it coincided with Miami Beach Pride weekend. But we shielded her from the general chaos that is Pride and did other touristy things around Miami and Biscayne Bay. We rode her on the Vespa, had dinner in Fort Lauderdale, and told her all about our new friends. It wasn't until the end of her trip when she said something about loving drag queens. I was completely floored. From then on, we knew we didn't have to dance around gay life anymore.

Mom opened our eyes with another remark that weekend. She told us that we were living our lives just like every other boring couple. I was happy that she arrived at that conclusion herself. I was pretty uptight about being gay back then, with more than a dose of conservative self-loathing. So I was committed to showing Mom that we were completely normal in our day-to-day lives— and not living like the screaming queen butler Agador Spartacus in the hit comedy film *The Birdcage*. Due to my profession, at the time I didn't want to be perceived as outwardly gay, for fear of professional repercussions and career roadblocks. It took some time to pull my head out of my ass about the straight-appearing gay masculinity issue.

We went house-shopping a few weekends in the Fort Lauderdale area with one of the coupled gays, who was a realtor and becoming a close friend. He and his partner, a psychiatrist, were lovely to be around and we had a lot in common. They also had dogs, enjoyed spending time by the pool, Saturday morning trips to area plant nurseries, and I loved our in-depth conversations over late night dinner creations. Sampson was attracted by a well-landscaped home in Wilton Manors. While the kitchen dimensions were smaller than I preferred, I relented and we went to see the house. We loved it immediately. It was well-cared-for, had a great backyard for the dog, a carport, enclosed laundry area, and was listed at a great price. Our offer on the home was accepted. We would close in July. We were thrilled to move closer to our friends and have a sense of community that accompanies living in a smaller neighborhood. The realtor and his partner would become our closest neighbors and friends of the entire Fort Lauderdale circle, plus Tom of course.

The next-door neighbor, Ron, was a gay retired IRS employee. Across the street were two gay men, and adjacent was an older gay man who loved twinks, specifically twinks who took advantage of elderly gays. I know this information because the police were called on multiple occasions to the home when one of the man's guests would steal from him. Ron would sit in his front yard sipping martinis and keep track of the gossip from the neighborhood. We were a mile from Wilton Drive, where the small city came alive. There were more bars per block than any other town. The average age in Wilton skewed higher than our age, so it was a great situation to be in. We were looked upon by locals as younger men—and therefore more attractive. Sampson and I went from being a Miami 5 to a Wilton 7.

On the day of the closing, USAA threw us a for a loop. We were at the closing table and some of the paperwork didn't reflect Sampson's name on the title and deed, as we had requested. Our mortgage handler hadn't been great, but this was a real issue—and at the worst possible time. Frantic phone calls were made and USAA told us that since the mortgage was a VA loan, Sampson couldn't be listed on the property. This was 2012, before the Defense of Marriage Act was overturned. Our marriage wasn't recognized in Florida and the LGBTQ community was still facing discriminatory practices. Sampson wanted to walk away from the deal, but we had no backup plan and a car full of our belongings in the driveway. Our closing agent figured out how to place the house into a trust and therefore list Sampson on the title and deed, so he would get the home in the event I died. Sampson didn't need to be on the loan, which was all USAA cared about, so it was fine. A few hours later, we officially closed. I swore I would never use USAA again.

In the midst of the home buying, the 2012 presidential campaign was in full swing. I had been assigned to a team. Our assignment was to travel to whatever city and state to serve as the security agents, also known as a post standers, for the presidential candidate coming to that venue. We were doing three weeks on the road at a time, three weeks back home. This went on for months. The money was great, as we worked lots of overtime. And whatever per diem I didn't use, I got to keep. This came in very handy for a couple that just purchased a new home. I was part of a Miami-based team. We drove all over Florida. But for some reason, we kept getting assignments in Ohio. Ohio is great and all, but three weeks there was a lot for me.

On one campaign stop in Cornfield, Ohio, we were the team for a campaign rally for Vice-President Joe Biden. I was assigned to make sure nobody accessed the stage until the VP arrived. While awkwardly facing the crowd, I was surprised when singer Jason Mraz walked out onstage to warm up the crowd. I was tickled that the guy I had watched sing karaoke years before was now a massive star. After his number, I tapped his arm and warmly told him he'd come a long way since Gus' Café more than ten years before. He looked befuddled; he had no idea who I was.

As the only gay agent on the jump team, I was stuck with whatever the heteros wanted to do after work. When I needed to break away, I often jogged solo. It was a great way to see the area and was a healthy habit. If we didn't have to be up early the next day, I would google local gay bars and visit. Otherwise, my team usually ended up at a mediocre Buffalo Wild Wings or Applebee's type restaurant. Dinners together could be entertaining, as we learned more about each other. Often, we focused on one another's vulnerabilities, which gave ammo for teasing each other. During one dinner in Nowhere, Florida, I learned something about myself. One of my peers filled me in that when I was brand-new to the office, a supervisor declared, "I don't want that faggot in my office!" So shortly thereafter I was reassigned to the airport squad. It's what I'd suspected all along!

I wasn't sure what to do with the information. I still didn't have career status, so I didn't have enough clout to lodge a formal complaint and be successful. It might have meant risking my career. I chose to keep my mouth shut.

I enjoyed the travel aspect of my job most, visiting places and meeting people I otherwise wouldn't have. Most of the time I was in another city, I was usually standing out of sight in some stairwell or next to a dumpster, but I was okay with that. Other times,

I would get to see things up close, like President Obama touring a salsa factory in Youngstown, Ohio or Mitt Romney attending a fundraiser in Boston. I was making good money for protecting Obama, Biden, Romney, and Paul Ryan on the campaign trail. But as seven months of duty continued in three-week rotations, I missed my husband and new friends. I wanted to go to sleep and wake up in our new home. I was becoming quite homesick, seeing the photos on social media of the weekend pool gatherings, boat rides, and evening outings on Wilton Drive. I had a brand-new home, a husband, and a new circle of friends—and I was unable to enjoy any of it. As my assignments grew longer, I didn't want Sampson to be sitting at home like a hermit; I encouraged him to socialize. My overtime and per diem from rotations were more than enough to give him the latitude to go out for dinners and clubbing. Sampson said he really only wanted to be with me.

Upon returning home from one of the final three-week rotations, I walked in the front door, hugged my husband, and began crying. The job had taken its toll. I wondered how much more stress I could take. But we sucked it up for another few weeks. I was able to fly home the day of the election and set my bags down for a while. We headed over to our friends' house to attend their election viewing party. I felt personally connected to the election, due to my attendance at countless presidential candidate rallies, campaign events, factory tours, and stump speeches. Obama had been doing a pretty good job of keeping the country on a decent path. But we had a lot on the line for this election, as the economy was still recovering from the shitstorm of the prior decade and LGBTQ rights still had work to be done. We all shared a giant sigh of relief when Obama was declared the winner.

CHAPTER SEVEN

NOW THAT THE ELECTION WAS behind me, I could focus on my life in Fort Lauderdale. I loved our house. It was only a two-bedroom but suited us well, since it had a good layout. The neighborhood was great. I went for runs all of the time out to Wilton Drive. Sampson eventually grew tired of the Fort Lauderdale to Miami commute, due to traffic mishaps – breakdowns, cars dropping furniture. He landed a job as an assistant to a realtor friend in Fort Lauderdale with a ton of properties. The realtor handled foreclosures, a really big business in South Florida. The realtor was overwhelmed by the paperwork and legwork involved. That's where Sampson came in. Once my husband got busy, the realtor's seventy properties quickly ballooned to over one hundred.

Regarding my Secret Service work, some sense of normalcy was setting in. I usually ended up only working one weekend a month, when a president from another country would visit South Florida. Or it was my weekend to work the Miami command center. I was enjoying life in Wilton Manors. We were growing closer to our circle of friends. There were still occasional hookups with friends and strangers, but there was no judgement. In our time together as friends, there was not one fight or dramatic episode. The group was hella fun and I loved our new family. We did dinners together and socialized on Wilton Drive. We shared pool parties, beach trips, weekend trips to Key West and Orlando, and vacationed together in Provincetown, MA. To be honest, I had no idea how many Ketel One cosmos we were consuming, but thankfully nobody ever got hurt and we kept the boozing confined to the weekends.

I was due to receive a pay raise at the start of 2013. We only had the Civic for Sampson's work mainly, so it made sense to buy another car. Sampson suggested the new Lexus GS350. The car was beautiful. It was fast for a larger luxury car and way more than we needed, but I loved it. Driving it home from the dealer, I underestimated the power in it. The rear end slid out while turning a corner. Thankfully, I recovered it, but it was a scare for driving a brand-new car. Our friends were all farther along in their careers and therefore more financially secure than we were, but I felt I needed to show them we belonged in the group by driving a car just as nice as the Audis they all drove. We could afford the car, but it was a poor decision on my part, based on insecurities.

Our Fort Lauderdale circle of friends were a family. We were there for each other. Included in the circle of friends was another couple, an older guy and a partner a good bit younger. The older guy was genuinely sweet and intelligent. We went to his house for a pool party one day. It was my first time there. Upon walking in his front door, I noticed a shelf with numerous awards on it, including multiple Grammy statuettes.

I was in pure shock. Our neighbor and friend was jazz royalty Gary Burton, and I didn't even know it. I always enjoyed his company and sitting and talking to him was always entertaining. I loved to hear his stories about touring and how he got to where he was, professionally and personally. I attended a few of his shows, at the Blue Note in Manhattan, in a jazz club in Georgetown, or when he played the Kennedy Center. To watch him in his element, as the music flowed through his body and to the instrument, was enamoring. Gary inspired me to get back into music, after hearing so much of his journey and his process for making music, I didn't feel it was too late for me, after all. I made a YouTube channel and uploaded videos of myself singing various songs. I had decided to video myself in the living room of our home and chose familiar songs I knew by heart, to simplify the recording. Due to the time that had lapsed since I had last played my guitar, it was more of a prop than anything in the videos. It was time-consuming and I needed total focus, which was hard to come by. I was concerned I would be too loud and the neighbors would be bothered, the cat or dog would interfere, or Sampson would come home and walk into the scene.

I had around 10,000 views on the videos prior to taking them down a few months later. I was again concerned my employer would learn of the videos and the potential fallout, even if it were just being teased by my peers.

I had posted an ad on Craigslist, seeking a band. The owner of Red Ridge Entertainment in Nashville contacted me. They were seeking talent to open for an act of theirs in South Florida. Additionally, I could fly to Nashville, record a six-song album, and they would assist with promoting and booking. All I needed was

$8,000. At the time, that was too much for me and I sought the advice of an attorney. I still carried the wounds of that first recording studio owner I had dealt with a decade prior. This one reached out to me and had provided more information, a possible gig, and showed up in Google searches. I felt better about this guy, but I never followed through, based on my 9 to 5 workload.

Work was going well, and I was flourishing in the counterfeit squad. My larger case, the counterfeit currency ring spanning across Florida, was gaining traction. The case had been growing for over a year and thousands of hours. Arrest by arrest, I was getting closer to the source. I was spending a lot of time in Palm Beach County. Since my direct supervisor was also acting supervisor of the West Palm Beach office, I had autonomy to pursue the case. I had forged a close relationship with a Delray Beach police detective and an analyst, which made for a great team. It was usually easier to obtain search warrants or warrants for vehicle tracking through the state and the detective had his thumb on the pulse of Delray, crucial to the investigation.

There were boring parts that accompany all investigations, like digging through paperwork, but the real fun was conducting surveillances from Miami to West Palm. It was a blast. We did trash pulls in the middle of the night and undercover work. I would get notifications the suspects were on the move and we would have to roll out at any hour to figure out where they were going.

At the time, I worked a couple of presidential protective division counterpart assignments and guarded lots of low-level foreign dignitaries that came to Miami. I was able to jump on a few car planes (the planes that carry the armored vehicles) in support of Obama or Biden, which took me to Singapore and Brazil. The flights were very long, due to multiple refueling stops, but Singapore was fun. Many of our Fort Lauderdale friends were Asian-Americans or men who preferred Asian men, so I had a growing appreciation for Asian cultures, as well as for how attractive the men could be. On that Singapore visit in early 2013, our car plane ended up breaking down and we got an additional day in Singapore until they could fix the plane. In the U.S. Air Force, a loadmaster is in charge of ensuring weight distributions are correct and the vehicles and gear are secure. An unsecured armored limo moving around at 40,000 feet can be dangerous and stall the aircraft while in flight. Prior to takeoff, I chatted up the loadmaster, discussing my experience fixing F-16s. As we headed into Thailand, the loadmaster invited me to the C-17 cockpit for the landing. It was amazing to see Thailand from that perspective and the envious faces of the other agents on board.

As the months passed, it was apparent Sampson was severely underpaid in his job—$25,000—and it was taking a toll on him. While the realtor had accumulated 120 properties, Sampson was doing all of the work to keep things organized. He was constantly on the go, from city halls to public utilities to banks to the properties themselves, dealing with the headache of foreclosed homes. Very rarely are homes in foreclosure turned over to the bank in pristine condition; for the realtor to sell the home, it entails some repair. The realtor took on properties all over Broward County, and Sampson was dealing with city employees who usually weren't willing to do much beyond the minimum. Sampson's boss was cheap and rolling in the profits. Sampson deserved better than that.

On one occasion, he came home from work visibly upset and went straight into the master bedroom, slamming the door. I went to talk to him but, through his tears, he refused to talk to me. I had never been shut out before. Sampson's response was counterintuitive to how I function; I see a problem and address it immediately. I let him be for a while.

Later, Sampson finally started talking. He confessed that he had gotten so down on himself, given his taxing career and his reliance on me. His self-worth was in the gutter. I was loving my career, but he was getting depressed in his. It was a watershed moment for us, and I knew things had to change.

At work, there had been a management rotation. The new powers that be seemed to genuinely care about the working agents. They went out of their way to come by and say hello, something the former boss never did. We were no longer saddled by the "good old boy" mentality that was embraced for a long time. I began to feel more secure in my job, especially since the new boss—a woman—had an open-door policy.

In early 2013, there was a push by the USSS to beef up personnel in Washington, D.C. and relocate agents. Given Sampson's work dilemma, this seemed a logical thing to apply for. Our families were in that region and it would be nice to live closer to them.

When I was originally hired, I was told I would be in the Miami Field Office for up to nine years. I was only at the three-year mark. I loved the Miami area, but a happy home life was paramount. It would be a good move to get to D.C. earlier than my classmates, as I was told after two years I could transfer to a permanent protective detail, shaving a year off of the normal timeline. It would also mean more job opportunities for Sampson, and we would have the protection of the District of Columbia recognizing our marriage. At that point, Sampson wasn't even on my insurance policies due to the discriminatory Defense of Marriage Act. So I talked to the big boss one day about our situation. I clearly made a strong case, because she promised to contact the person who handles reassignments.

In July 2013, the Supreme Court overturned DOMA, granting the LGBTQ community a massive win. I could finally provide Sampson with all of the job benefits I had enjoyed for years and alleviate those fiscal concerns. Since I was a federal employee, they would now have to recognize Sampson as my legal spouse, which was a BFD (big fucking deal). I contacted our benefits department to get Sampson onto my insurance plans. They were completely unprepared, warning me it would take some time for directives to filter down from the Office of Professional Management. I'm not sure why I thought the U.S. federal government would have been prepared for this. As it turned out, I was the first gay agent to begin this process. While I was a bit apprehensive, I felt empowered by the SCOTUS decision and continued pushing the issue until it was resolved.

As the summer passed, the rumors were flying high that I would get sent to D.C. early. The offer was framed like this: Come to the Washington Field Office for two years and then you can proceed to the second part of your career, which was called phase two. Phase two is the meat and potatoes of the USSS. That is, it's where it all comes together: To protect the President, Vice-President, their families, and other important people. The move would put me a year ahead of my classmates. Upon completing four years on a protective detail, I would rotate back into the field, ideally choosing where to ride out my remaining years with the agency. Sampson and I were all for it. For Sampson's career, his well-being, and our aspirations to have a family, getting back to the Northeast made sense.

While at the United Nations convention in September in New York City, I received the phone call from the Special Agent in Charge: I would be transferring to Washington in January 2014. She had followed through on her word. Sampson was ecstatic. To top it off, the government would be paying for the move and most related expenses, like realtor fees, movers, and the house-hunting trip.

We now had four months to get our home sold, find a new home, and relocate to the DC area. We broke the news to our Fort Lauderdale gay family. It would be upsetting to leave them all behind. We used our realtor friend to list our home. The housing market was swinging in our favor. The government would be paying our friend's six percent in realtor fees and we'd walk away with more in our pockets, which would be desperately needed to buy a home in DC. The house wasn't listed more than a week before we had a full-priced offer. Given we'd only owned the home for less than two years, it had appreciated twenty-five percent during a recovering economy (Thanks, Obama!). Closing was a lot sooner than expected and we had to find temporary housing, since my report date to Washington was January 10, 2014.

The moving company showed up in October 2013 with a tractor trailer and packed and loaded everything for us, including Gloria the Vespa. It was sad to walk away from our cute little home.

A coworker offered up his parent's townhome in the Victoria Park neighborhood for our temporary home, since they lived in Louisiana and only used the home when they visited. We were incredibly fortunate to have such good friends supporting us through the transition. Prior to deciding on relocation, we had signed up and already paid to go on our first Atlantis cruise with our Fort Lauderdale gay family. We planned to fly back to South Florida at the end of January for the cruise.

Our final months in Fort Lauderdale were bittersweet. Things got real when the gang got together for our annual Thanksgiving gathering. Emotions ran high during this last big chosen family dinner. Every year, we all gathered for Thanksgiving, sometimes there would be forty people there. Everyone knew we were moving and during photos at the end of the dinner, I cried as I hugged our closest friends. Only a few weeks remained until we would be a thousand miles apart. In early December, we went to DC for our house-hunting trip. I had booked our flights through the USSS travel agency, only to have Sampson's tickets suddenly cancelled. His ticket was not valid since he was a man. I was livid and immediately began calling the powers that be to rectify this situation. This was now the second time where I was the first married gay agent denied benefits that heterosexual couples had enjoyed for years. Similar to the health insurance debacle a few months prior, there wasn't a company policy on how to handle a same-sex married couple regarding house-hunting and relocation benefits. It only took a few days for them to realize they were violating law and to fix the situation. We had only ten days to find our next home, so the pressure was on. We had our budget, pre-approval letter, and a general idea as to what we wanted.

On our second day out with our realtor in DC, Sampson saw a new building at 11th Street and V Street NW near Columbia Heights, set to open soon. A call was made, and we went to see the condo. The occupancy permit had not yet been issued, so nobody lived in the building. We walked into a second-floor unit and inspected the layout, the ambient sunlight, the bay window overlooking V Street, and the private balcony. We loved it. We made an offer and, voila, we were under contract on day two! The rest of the trip was spent with family and friends in Richmond, Virginia.

Back at the Miami Field Office, I had to focus on my counterfeit investigation in the time I had remaining. I'd had a bunch of arrests up until that point and all signs pointed to a prior USSS counterfeit arrestee as one of the sources. We stepped up our game and obtained enough evidence to secure a federal arrest warrant for the suspect. We arrested him without incident. Given the amount of information I'd obtained on him, it would be difficult to talk his way out of it. We also had the added weight of him being a repeat offender when it came time for sentencing before a federal judge. I was able to secure a confession from the subject, in the presence of his attorney. He spilled the beans on his co-conspirator, in hopes of a lighter sentence. Before I left, I passed the case on to a newer agent—and prayed that he wouldn't mess up two years of work. The only thing left to do was obtain a search warrant for the co-conspirators' abode, seize the counterfeiting operation, and arrest him. I had a sense of accomplishment as all of this transpired. It was my first large case and the first time my work product, as a Special Agent, was able to speak for itself. My boss was extremely pleased, and it made me feel more confident in my role, not only as an equal but be seen as a successful agent. It was very close to

Christmas and trying to get things done in the government around that time is pointless, since most people take off the last two weeks of the year so the final arrest and search warrant were delayed.

Once I was in DC, I received a call from my former boss. The counterfeit plant was seized, and the co-conspirator arrested. At that time, there was over four million dollars' worth of counterfeit currency generated by these two individuals. I felt a sense of relief, that two years' worth of hard work and dedication had paid off and I now had a successful case under my belt. I was just as good of an agent as my peers. I felt I had to prove to everyone that I deserved to be there, and my sexuality didn't matter.

My last trip for the Miami Field Office was as a member of the advance team to the Dominican Republic for the Clintons, which fell over New Year's Eve. It was a beautiful place to be, but I ended up watching the Times Square ball drop from the TV in my hotel room by myself. Feeling lonely, I had to remind myself this was what I had signed up to do. I tried to keep in mind how fortunate I was, to not wallow in my solitude.

In early January, Sampson and I loaded the car for the twelve-hour drive to DC. We had flown my dog Baxter to a friend in Richmond to look after until we were settled in, so it was just the two of us and Leslie, the cat. Our first stop was in Jacksonville to stay with friends for a night. The trip wasn't easy, since I'd thrown a disc in my lower back a few months prior, during a CrossFit workout. The pain radiated down my left leg almost constantly, even after three spinal injections, and ruined my sleep. I could hardly walk one hundred yards without having to stop and bend down to ease the pain. Surgery was the next option.

We arrived in DC and awaited our closing date and the final paperwork. Until the District issued the occupancy permit, the Veterans Administration couldn't approve the condo building or loan. It finally happened—a day before we were to close on the condo and movers were scheduled to arrive. We drove to the settlement company in the middle of a snowstorm and our realtor instructed us to wait next door in a coffee shop while a delay on the part of the attorney was being resolved. But soon the attorney walked into the coffee shop and told us he was quitting his job and then he walked out. We had no idea what to do other than laugh. Our closing had to happen, and we waited it out for a couple of hours until the settlement company found another attorney who could handle the closing. I recalled how our prior home closing involved similar melodrama.

The movers arrived the next day. Our new Crate & Barrel sofa wouldn't fit through the front door. The movers debated removing windows and hoisting it up, but we decided just to sell it and avoid the mess. We rapidly unpacked the condo and a day later, I reported for my first day in the office for orientation. I was in the office for two days, obtained my access cards, government vehicle (a busted old blue Ford Taurus we nicknamed Grandma), and a quick meet-and-greet with my supervisors. I was told by classmates who had been in the office since training that the office was a beast. If you didn't take time for yourself, they warned, it would eat you alive. A couple of days later, Sampson and I packed our bags for a week-long cruise. This made me feel less guilty about going on the cruise we had booked and paid for months ago, days after showing up in the new office.

We landed in Fort Lauderdale and stayed with our friends before the cruise departed. This was a new experience for us, but our friends had been on Atlantis cruises before, so they filled us in. Our group coordinated outfits for each themed party scheduled. There's a rule on cruise ships where each passenger can bring a bottle of wine or champagne on board. So we bought a ton of Veuve Clicquot plus Ketel One vodka. A limo van drove ten of us to the port, with another fifteen friends meeting us at there. I felt a palpable excitement since I had never been on a cruise. Once we were on board the Celebrity Silhouette and the muster drill was done, we met on the top deck for the traditional sail away ritual.

I was with close friends on a boat full of gay men, booze was about to flow endlessly, and even my cell phone was off. I had no responsibilities for seven days. What could go wrong? It was a euphoric feeling.

We scoped out the ship, planning where to meet up at night for dancing, and which bartenders we could lubricate with tips to get better service. We all went to dinner, which was challenging to try and coordinate with twenty-five people. We quickly found it was easier to break the party into smaller groups and let them sort it out. The main dinner was nice, but the courses were heavier in nature and eating took twice as long. I get fidgety when I have a plan in my head and the timing doesn't go as planned, so after dinner I took a nap, so we could meet up at 10:30pm to pregame. Our room was connected to our closest coupled friends, which allowed us to create a central staging area to put on our coordinated costumes. When twenty-five outrageous queens step out in the same threads, it makes for an entrance.

The first night on the Celebrity Silhouette was surreal; I'd never experienced anything like it in my life. We were on a dance floor in the middle of the ocean with a sound system that reverberated through your body, a light show shooting beams as far as the eye could see, and beautiful men in costumes. I felt the energy of acceptance and love. I don't use any drugs except for alcohol, but I had no problem dancing every night until 7:00 AM.

There was a schedule of moderation you had to follow in order to survive the week. I'd wake up around noon, eat, relax on the pool deck, then change into coordinated outfits for the afternoon tea dance. After a post-tea dance shower, I would change and eat dinner, have a disco nap, pregame again, and dance from 11pm to 7:00 AM. Once back in my cabin, I would order room service, then crash.

This intense routine went on for seven days. Not once did I have a hangover or get sick and my back pain that had plagued me for several months was miraculously gone. I learned that you can make the cruise whatever you want to make it. If you want to seek out the boys, then there's a lot to choose from. Or you can be in bed by 10:00 PM each night. We decided to walk the middle line and decided we would play with other another guy or couple, as a couple, when it felt right. It was commonplace on the ship for this to occur, so it made sense to partake. After all, we had not experienced any negative outcomes from prior hookups. We would be on the dance floor and someone would dance his way in between us and we would hook up in a three-way. That's how the week went. Or we would meet a flirty boy in the hall, or we'd receive messages on the whiteboard. I felt as though I was in a parallel dimension, where the societal constraints usually placed on us were cast aside. On the ship, everyone felt comfortable enough to be their true selves without judgement.

By mid-week, Sampson was turning in a little earlier than I was.

He was usually the one to desire more sleep, even at home, and he had some introvert tendencies, whereas I was the opposite. That is, he would go to bed around 3:00 AM while I would dance until daybreak. I rationalized my wildness this way: We'd paid a lot to be on the cruise and I wanted to get my money's worth. One night, Tom called our cabin from the martini bar. He asked us to meet him for a drink. Once we arrived, he introduced us to two guys from DC—David and Keith, a long-term couple who lived near our new home. David and Keith both worked for the federal government. They were also avid cruisers. We instantly connected with them on a friendship level. David was a keen listener and Keith was a keen observer full of wit; they blended perfectly with our Fort Lauderdale family for the rest of the cruise.

On the last night at sea, I felt sad. We had a final dinner together and said goodbye to our Fort Lauderdale family. We disembarked the next morning and flew home to Washington, D.C., to begin the next chapter in our lives.

CHAPTER EIGHT

WE ARRIVED BACK HOME FROM the cruise to our brand-new condo. My dog was in Richmond, VA and we had to find time to go get him. Sampson was again unemployed due to the relocation and trying to find his way forward professionally. We hoped the DC job market would be a far better fit for him than South Florida had been.

When I reported to the Washington Field Office (WFO). I was assigned to the counterfeit squad, again. That bothered me; I preferred new career challenges that would utilize other skillsets. I quickly learned that the criminal squads in WFO were nothing more than professional post standers. That is, we were the agents that were pulled to work the endless flow of protective visits that DC demands. Since the President, Vice-President, their families, and other USSS protected persons lived in the DC area, the assignments never ended. Given the job demands, I realized there would be no way I could work a significant criminal investigation. But after that huge case in Miami, I didn't mind the break. One agent (an old classmate) was exempt from most protection assignments since he was working a large counterfeit case and I began to assist him as he needed between protection assignments. And he needed major help. When I wasn't standing next to a dumpster, in front of a door in the subfreezing temperatures, or in a stairwell for ten hours, I was assisting the case agent with his investigation. Whether it was processing evidence, monitoring the surveillance, or pestering the Assistant U.S. Attorney, all hands-on deck were required to bring the case to a close. That case ended up being the largest counterfeit case at that time, with fraud losses north of 70 million dollars.

There was a running joke among my academy training classmates, taking bets on who would be the next to leave the Secret Service for a more stable life. When my WFO peer heading the counterfeit case left, we were down to fifteen agents left on the job. Most of my classmates had gone to other federal agencies. A few went in totally different directions outside of law enforcement, from starting a landscaping company to practicing law.

I received a text message in June 2014. After working a midnight shift in Chicago, my classmate Jim, my friend from the academy, went to the gym. Jim was a phenomenally nice guy, a Marine, and father to two sons. While he was working out, he had a sudden massive heart attack. (He was the one who was strong as an ox, but always smoking.) He died en route to the hospital. I was at a loss for words. I had seen him a couple of months prior during a weekend trip to Chicago, where we went for dinner and caught up. He was excited for his future with his girlfriend and had been spending more time with his kids, after a messy divorce. All of It was gone in an instant.

My supervisor approved my time off from work to attend the funeral services. Arrangements were made for Jim to be laid to rest near Erie, PA, where he was originally from. I met up with TJ, a woman friend from the academy who also knew him, to begin the trek north. My grandparents were along the route, offering a pleasant detour from the sad journey. A couple of members from headquarters also made the drive north.

I'll give kudos to the service; when it comes to taking care of each other, we show up. There were four of us from our class at the funeral. We sat stoically during the service, but my eyes were usually on his children and girlfriend, all of whom I had met before. I couldn't fathom the grief they felt, to have everything upended without notice. I approached his loved ones, passing my condolences, and walked outside. I didn't want to prolong their grieving during such a personal moment in their lives. Afterwards we went to dinner together at a nearby Friendly's restaurant. It was great to reminisce, catch up, and laugh a little, which is what Jim would have wanted us to do. On the way back to DC, we stopped at my grandparents' house. My grandfather was very confused. He stared at TJ, a tall, African- American woman, throughout the visit. When it came time to leave, TJ went to shake his hand, but my grandfather suddenly pulled her in for a hug and told her she was getting to be just as big as her dad. My grandfather, who was in his mid-90s, didn't hug anyone. It wasn't his style. We awkwardly walked out, asking what the hell just happened. Maybe he thought TJ was my child? We just shrugged and laughed.

Early in my tenure at WFO, I was working a visit for a high-level foreign dignitary. We had gone to the World Bank in DC. I was stationed at the elevator to ensure it remained available. There was a representative from the building's management team stationed as the designated elevator operator.

She and I were chatting. I can talk to a brick wall, as I'm an extrovert. Besides, working in law enforcement teaches you to interact with total strangers. The woman was a property manager for the well-known commercial property management company that managed the building. I had told her my husband and I were new to the DC area, mentioning Sampson's work for the realtor in South Florida. She told me they planned to hire an assistant property manager and maybe Sampson might be a good fit. He submitted his resume and was hired.

Sampson was soon making a decent salary with benefits, with the opportunity of upward mobility with the company. I thought back to all the pain, stress, and worry he had experienced for his career while living in South Florida. Upon landing his new job, Sampson wanted to add a member to the family. So he bought the new Vespa Primavera in dark blue one to accompany Gloria, our red one. Riding the Vespas around DC was great. We would find backroads to ride to Virginia and Maryland or just ride around the National Mall. It was a way for us to connect and share in something we both loved.

Living right off of U Street NW in DC was a lot of fun. It was a couple of blocks to the bars and our condo often served as a pregaming location before a night out on the town with friends. Sampson and I had begun hanging out with Keith and David, and meeting their circle of friends, most in government service. Sampson's best friend Doug had also moved from Richmond, Virginia to DC. It was a seamless transition for us and I never felt the void, like we did upon arriving in Miami, when it came to making new friends. We also had the assistance of gay apps to meet new neighbors. Following our time in Fort Lauderdale, I found myself more attracted to Asian men since our circle of friends had been comprised of mixed-race couples, Asian men and white men. Online, I was chatting with a tall athletic Chinese American guy on Grindr, who I found very attractive. I met Tony for coffee. But I immediately knew there would not be a hookup; we kept it on a friendship level. A hookup was easy to come by, but finding good friends is not, and I was smart enough to recognize it.

The neighborhood Sampson and I lived in was relatively safe; we had only one shooting on the block while we lived there. Any recurring problems stemmed from bar hoppers drinking in their cars and throwing their bottles in the yard of our condo building or pissing on our garage. At the end of their partying, they were obnoxiously loud and discarded their 3:00 AM pizza boxes in the street. Our condo was on the second floor, so we heard everything.

Not long after we moved in, we began a Sunday ritual of picking up litter from around our building and the blocks nearby. In South Florida, people cared for their neighborhood, so I expected the same in DC. A few people thanked us for pitching in, but most ignored us. But that didn't stop the trash from accumulating again. Eventually we realized we were only wasting our own time. Some aspects of city living were a pain in the ass.

Sampson and I realized our five-year wedding anniversary was approaching. Since we didn't celebrate a honeymoon, we decided to take an anniversary trip to London and Paris to mark the occasion. We found a boutique hotel in the SoHo section of London and, at the suggestion of our friend, booked a suite at Hotel Rouge near the Seine River in Paris. We booked flights via British Airways, landed in London, and took in the city. I arranged a tour of the Tower of London through our USSS office there, but we were winging the rest of the trip.

We must have walked a dozen miles every day, exploring and wandering. At night, we made sure to go out to the gay bars to get a feel for the scene. While dancing on the elevated dance area at the dance club GAY, somebody shoved me, causing me to fall off of the dance area. I looked up but did not know who had pushed me or why, sobering me up rapidly. Had I committed a faux pas? Sampson and I were always cognizant to avoid being the stereotypical rude Americans and respect a foreign culture. One night out, we were at one of the SoHo bars. I was dancing with a dark wavy-haired local who asked if we wanted to hang out afterward. Sampson and I were still open to extracurricular fun, so we brought him back to our hotel for a nightcap. But the front desk had a strict rule against unregistered guests, and we awkwardly sent the chap on his way.

We were excited to get to Paris for the allure of the city. It's where my family emigrated to America in 1910. We checked into the hotel, in the Premiere Arrondissement, then began our foot tour of the City of Lights. We were in one of the most romantic cities, and thought I would be overwhelmed with love and romanticism, but something inside of me felt off. It didn't feel like we were as connected as we should have been, something was amiss between us. Sampson's behavior wasn't any different than usual, I just felt disconnected from him. I was saddened to feel this way, for I was with my husband on our five-year anniversary. I felt an internal strife, one I could not describe. I was afraid to let my husband inside my head, since even I didn't fully understand the problem.

It was a city full of beautiful people, including the most attractive men. We walked all over creation, taking photos, buying lockets, and dining enjoying the sidewalk cafes. We had made anniversary reservations to have lunch at the Eiffel Tower. The place had employed a stunning elevator operator. He was tall, had dark hair, and bright blue eyes with a sly smile that had a hint of flirtatiousness. You may think I'm a total dick to notice a hot guy while on an anniversary trip with my husband. But we had been together so long that we generally knew each other's tastes and we would discuss men openly. Sampson noticed the elevator operator's smile in my direction, as well as his lovely lips, and teased me about him.

The lunch was fantastic, with numerous courses and champagne. We winced to see other American couples complaining about the food and service and being general assholes to waitstaff. The lunch cost over $300 but was worth the experience. On our way out of the Eiffel Tower, I considered inviting the elevator operator out that night, Sampson was open to it, but I decided against it, since it was our anniversary. We went out at night into Le Marais (the gayborhood) and were sure to visit RAIDD bar for its nude shower shows. Even if I weren't into every guy showering, I couldn't help but stand and stare. After barhopping through the area, we stopped for some sandwiches to sober up en route to the hotel.

On our final night in town, we went to CUD, one of the gay bars in Le Marais. We had a couple of drinks and wandered among the crowd for a while, at times apart. Just as we were leaving, something went off inside of me, prompting a deep and uncontrollable sobbing. I could not stop. My gut was telling me something was very wrong in my relationship. Trying to console me, Sampson asked me what was wrong. But I couldn't put my emotions into thoughts or my thoughts into words.

Once the tears ran dry, we went for sandwiches and ate them in front of a beautiful museum. I felt better now. But my uncontrollable outburst still troubled me. I was afraid to share my suspicions with Sampson, that I feared for our own relationship. Because I was afraid he would confirm my fears—and I felt that would be even worse.

I was used to being in control at all times in my life. I had operated this way for over a decade in my career. Why was I not feeling in control anymore? I asked myself if what I was feeling was jealousy, because I didn't like how our relationship had changed and how we were becoming more liberated from each other sexually. I wondered if it stemmed from Sampson becoming more independent from me, and how I was afraid I was losing him.

I had all of these different thoughts and fears swirling in my mind, but I didn't have the tools to understand them all. Even worse was that I had put up a wall to prevent Sampson from understanding the depth of the issues—a wall that prevented him from even helping me. Instead of letting him in, I reverted back to my classic role, as the stoic and strong husband—the role I thought I was supposed to play. We didn't discuss the issue again.

In early 2015, I was paroled from the counterfeit squad and transferred to the Protective Intelligence squad. The new job meant I was less likely to stand in the freezing cold for endless hours. The intelligence agents were responsible for interviewing people who requested to speak to the President, those who sought to harm any USSS protectee, or circumvent USSS security. The White House often seemed a magnet for those who were mentally ill. I had a lot of exposure to such people as a police officer, especially individuals who were threatening to harm themselves or others. My task was to deescalate the situation, identify if a threat was present, and get them treatment. There is an ongoing stigma associated with mental illness and that causes people to avoid seeking the treatment they need, which only makes their condition worse.

There were some days we'd get call after call about people who had approached a Uniform Division Officer. We'd have to assess if this person was a threat to any Secret Service protected person, themselves, or the general public, while mitigating the risk and resolving the matter. It was a ridiculously busy squad to be in. We were required to work all shifts, holidays, and weekends, as the mission required it, with the upside being bountiful overtime. This was due to a manpower shortage in our agency, and we felt the effects more than most in the Washington Field Office. We had been losing agents left and right, who sought a more normal and balanced work life. Hiring and training new agents was an extensive process that took at least a year. In our squad, we were ranked by seniority and morale was in the gutter. One of my squad mates quit cold turkey. He turned in his equipment and walked away to be a stay-at-home father while others networked to transfer to other Special Agent positions or agencies.

The Secret Service was undergoing a lot of painful changes and we were bearing the brunt of it, always being told it would get better. As this routine of staff attrition and overtime wore on, we were getting worn down. The longest stretch I went without a day off was two months. I couldn't plan anything, and I couldn't be there for my husband who was now flourishing in his career. My guilt was somehow lessened by the knowledge that his best friend Doug was nearby, and Sampson had lots of other friends in the area. But my personal life was dwindling before my eyes and I felt trapped. I felt I had no avenue out, other than to quit. I had never been more unhappy with my professional career.

At WFO, I had been warned early on that the beast never sleeps. We went from one giant assignment to the next. The intensity was omnipresent. The Secret Service has a zero-fail mission and the men and women who wore the badge never forgot it. Unfortunately, the Service rewards hard workers with more work, meaning the best workers are driven into the ground.

My next big assignment was the September 2015 visit of Pope Francis to Washington, DC. The visit had been deemed a National Security Special Event, which triggers additional funding and assets. It was another all-hands-on-deck assignment for WFO. I chose to be a site agent for the Pope's parade route, so a section would be my responsibility. I would coordinate with law enforcement partners to ensure thousands of spectators were screened and which facilities and route would be cordoned off, so the Pope could move safely. It was a massive undertaking that required our agents work seamlessly together. I lost count of the number of meetings I had to attend.

The evening before the visit, Pennsylvania Avenue was shut down so the buildout could begin. I was present to ensure the fencing, barriers, facilities, screening areas were all being put into place. We were expecting tens of thousands of onlookers to line the streets of DC and it was up to us to ensure none of them were dangerous, nor had the opportunity to get near the Pope. I worked until midnight. After a couple of hours of sleep, I returned to the route at 4:00 AM to resume work.

My zone encompassed the Washington Monument, Smithsonian's African American Museum, and the National Mall, which meant these massive structures also had to be secured. The media staging area was in my zone, adding an extra layer of scrutiny to everything I did, since I'd be on live feed cameras most the day. As gameday progressed, things had fallen into place. There wasn't much else I could do but wait for the Pope to roll by in his Pope-mobile. It was the largest event I'd ever worked as a site agent. It was exactly what I signed up to do as a Special Agent.

The Pope finally arrived to my zone, then slowly rolled through. And that was it. Months of planning for a few minutes' worth of showtime. Later that day, I received countless texts from loved ones and friends who had seen me on live TV, which was a fun feeling.

As the 2016 campaign got underway, I was assigned to handle a protective visit for Hillary Clinton to the CNN news bureau in DC. I was happy to see the inner workings of a large newsroom. Wolf Blitzer walked by, much shorter than I expected. And then he appeared, the gay icon and silver daddy, the object of lust for millions of gay men. Anderson Cooper would be handling the interview. It occurred without incident.

Work was over, but I couldn't let the opportunity pass. Anderson was one of the very few celebrities I'd always wanted to meet. He had been a constant in my life since high school and he always presented himself on screen as genuine—with an adorable giggle. He was a piece of history, given who his blueblood, high society parents were. I asked an assistant if Cooper would be willing to take a photo. She introduced us and this Secret Service Agent went all schoolgirl. Eventually I was able to explain what an honor it was to meet him.

Cooper was kind and recalled how Secret Service agents would accompany the Reagans to his family's Upper East Side townhouse in the 1980s and how he admired the agents' work. He was happy to pose for a photo, pulling me in closer than I'd anticipated. He was sweet and kind, and I was thrilled to meet him.

During one assignment in early 2016, six years into my time as an agent, I was in the area of the White House, waiting on Vice-President Biden to leave the area. I was sitting in the car with the windows down, talking with my colleague, when I heard someone yell, "Drop the gun, drop the gun!" followed by a gunshot.

The shot was fired within close proximity to where we were. As a Protective Intelligence agent, I knew the situation was about to end up in our laps. I jumped out of the truck, grabbed whatever gear I could, and headed in the direction of the gunshot. The incident had taken place only fifty yards from where we were parked, and things were still happening when I got there. The subject was handcuffed and officers began tending to his gunshot injuries. My police officer experience kicked in and I tasked a uniformed officer to begin a crime scene log. Within moments there was a flood of people pouring into the area and we had to maintain control. Senior level management arrived and a high-ranking member of WFO management assigned the investigation to me. I felt overwhelmed and immediately called a senior agent in our squad to come assist me. As the case agent, I was the USSS representative for the endless meetings that would later be held with the numerous federal and DC law enforcement partners involved. I was surprised to be trusted to represent our agency on such a sensitive issue, but also happy. Needless to say, the investigation occupied most of my time for a while. I was attending briefings, meetings, interviews, collecting as much information as possible and writing long reports. Thankfully, as RuPaul warns, I didn't fuck it up.

During this time, my dog Baxter, who was eleven, suffered a seizure while we were out for a walk. He recovered and we continued home. I was alarmed and frightened to see him have a seizure that severe, in the middle of traffic and it completely incapacitated him. Later that night, he suffered another seizure. But this time, he wouldn't stop seizing. I grabbed him and headed to the ER by myself. Baxter had experienced minor seizures in the past, but this was far more serious. At the ER, doctors injected him with a drug to stop the seizure. They held him overnight for observation. The next day, when I returned to get Baxter, the vet said he had suffered cluster seizures through the evening, and that meds would be a permanent part of his future.

When I got Baxter home, I realized he had suffered a stroke. He wandered the condo endlessly, only making right turns. His vision had also been affected, and he had lost bladder control. I called my primary veterinarian and agreed to meet in the morning if things didn't improve. Sampson slept in the master bedroom with the door closed so he could be rested for work the next morning and he was never attached to Baxter anyhow. I slept on the sofa that night so I could keep an eye on my child, since Baxter was still wandering around all night. I stayed up with him.

The morning sun rose, and I called the vet to let her know we would be coming in. We began the painful walk to Fourteenth

Street. Upon examining Baxter, she agreed with the ER vet that the best course of action was to end his pain. As I held Baxter, I told him repeatedly that I loved him. She administered the medicine and his body soon relaxed in my arms. I kissed his head and held him until the vet told me he was over the rainbow bridge. I was sobbing a lot, for Baxter had been with me for over eleven years, up and down the East Coast. He was a loyal, loving, and obedient dog who gave me much happiness; I only hope I did the same for him.

CHAPTER NINE

IN THE MIDST OF ALL OF THE work obligations, Sampson and I had begun to think about how to make our family bigger. My mentality was there is no perfect time to have kids and my biological clock was ticking, despite the lack of ovaries, so I lobbied hard for it. Sampson had claimed he also desired children, so it seemed like the appropriate next step. I tried to push aside two unresolved issues: the demands of my job and my nagging concerns about our relationship that had caused me agony in Paris. Having children has always been a dream of mine and given we had good stable incomes, a new condo, and friends and family in proximity, it seemed like the right time to venture down that path.

We had done some homework and found surrogacy for one child to be roughly $100,000. Then there was the dilemma of deciding whose DNA we would use. My sister had volunteered to carry a child for us, as she's that type of amazing person. If she were to donate her egg and carry the child, we could use Sampson's DNA to father the child. Therefore, it would be biologically related to both of us and resemble us, since my sister and I look similar. My fear of using this method, however, was that my sister had blood pressure complications when she delivered her second daughter. The risk was too great for me, so I graciously declined her offer.

Our next option was adoption. My maternal grandfather had adopted and fostered all of his children. This seemed like a logical fit and a way to honor the sacrifices my grandparents had made decades earlier. We researched area adoption agencies and narrowed our search.

We chose a local non-profit adoption agency in Bethesda, Maryland, attended an information meeting, and decided to use them. I had assumed adopting a child would be low- cost, but I was wrong. The fees were based on a sliding scale. Given our incomes, we'd be paying around $50,000 to adopt a baby. We decided to proceed. We had to fill out an insane amount of paperwork, which was far more intrusive than my security clearance documents at work. There would be three home visits, even before being approved for a child. The social worker interviewed us together and separately. I had a small concern the social worker would discover we had an open marriage and toss us from the program, but it never came up. Since they also obtain your medical records, I also had to explain why I was on Truvada while in a monogamous relationship. I told her I took the medication to lower my risk of contracting HIV when dealing with mentally ill persons in the course of work. She didn't question my alibi.

The home study process took six months and thousands of dollars in fees, but we were eventually approved. We had to travel to Buffalo, New York, where a partnering agency located mothers who were seeking to have their child adopted. We attended the additional training in Buffalo and that was the final step in what had become a nerve-racking process. At the time, we had a Toyota Prius that was practical, but I felt the need to upgrade to something safer for a family. I went to Toyota and came home with a new 4Runner Limited. I'll admit that it was a freak-out purchase, but I did love the truck and knew my family would be higher off the ground.

Life in WFO continued, including work at nights, weekends, holidays, and for weeks without a day off. But the overtime pay was helpful in paying for adoption expenses. The wait for a call from the adoption agency could be a week away or two years away, we had no way of knowing.

In early 2016, we flew to South Florida and reunited with our friends to embark on another Atlantis cruise. We'd really enjoyed the first cruise. Our group was a little smaller on the second cruise, but the ship was twice as big—5,000 gays on one big floating circuit party. The euphoric feelings weren't quite as strong this time. Sampson was different than he was two years prior. He had begun to pass up parties and went to bed a lot earlier than me. I had felt the distancing, hence my tears during our Paris trip. But I went back to ignoring reality because I didn't want to face it.

The weather was cooler on the ship that year, so our group would huddle up, drink quickly, and then get to the dancefloor to warm up. Once again, I stayed up all night dancing away. During that time, I was introduced to a tall Taiwanese guy who had abs for days and lived in Chicago. Kai and I spent a lot of time together that week, both in bed and out, and it was obvious to everyone. Since Sampson and I were spending time apart on the ship, and we had liberty to play, I focused my attentions and sexual energy on this friendly stranger. The fun we had was in stark contrast to the almost sexless relationship I had with Sampson.

When the cruise came to an end, Sampson was happy to get back home. But I wanted the fun to continue. I realized I wanted to spend more time with Kai, even though he was back in Chicago. I wanted to continue to be in the alternate reality of the ship. A place where work demands didn't exist. A place that celebrated freedom and liberation. A place where the sexual attention was electric. That world was far more attractive than the reality where I was married to my job and sought sexual gratification from inviting extras into the bedroom.

Kai and I remained in contact after the cruise, via text and Facetime, and even meeting up once in New York City when we were both visiting at the same time, rekindling the cruise romps one more time. A month later, I came to my senses. I was a married man and though we had an open relationship, I knew my focus needed to be on my own situation at home. I decided that the passionate week at sea was over and I had fond memories. But I pledged that we should simply remain friends and it was not feasible to seek out anything more than that. Kai was on the same page since his life was blossoming in Chicago.

As the spring of 2016 wore on, Sampson was more unhappy in the city, we talked about moving out to Virginia. It would be safer, I decided, for our growing family. We decided to look for a place in Arlington or Alexandria. Our realtor assured us our DC condo would have no issues getting sold. It was quickly snatched up by a former ambassador—in cash—for her son. However, we had to be out of the condo in three weeks. Meanwhile, Sampson had found a new development in the Potomac Yard area of Alexandria. The units were quality-built, well-priced and high-end. We decided on a 3,000-square-foot, two-story condo at the very end of the neighborhood overlooking a park. I wanted to keep Sampson happy and the guilt I carried from the demands of my job added to my over-eagerness to keep him happy by spending money. So I threw cash and material goods at our relationship, despite the significant red flags in front of my eyes. The Virginia move wasn't something he demanded or pressured me into; I was doing what I thought I should be doing, to my own detriment. This was all transpiring in a presidential campaign year, and I had already been traveling out three weeks at a time since January. Since our new condo wouldn't be ready until late June, Sampson arranged to stay with Doug in downtown DC. It would save us a ton of money, provide Sampson company in my absence, since I was never home.

The Secret Service work for the 2016 campaign would be a large undertaking, given President Obama would be on the campaign trail for Hillary Clinton a lot. Each campaign is different, just as every protectee and protective site is. However, in my view, Trump brought an aura of unknown since he wasn't the standard politician. I chose to be a Jump Team Leader, as I was a member in 2012 for the campaign. A jump team leader is assigned to travel the country with a team of agents, whom they are responsible for, and serving as the venue security team when a presidential candidate visits some place. I wanted the leadership experience for my resume. Being a jump team leader involved little paperwork and lots of travel (i.e., overtime and per diem). They tell you where to go with the team, where to stand, and for how long.

The campaign quickly kicked into high gear. Like 2012, I'd be on the road for three weeks and then home for three weeks. Early in the campaign, the Service was covering Ben Carson, Bernie Sanders, Trump, Hillary, and the sitting President, Vice-President, and their families. On one assignment, I was assigned to North Carolina to serve as a site agent. But after driving there, I found the assignment was cancelled. (Schedules change all the time.) I was then sent to Charleston, South Carolina, to serve as a shift agent for Ben Carson. I was now a considerable distance from DC and in my government vehicle, by myself. This was not ideal and limited where I could be sent and what roles I could fill during a campaign year. They tried to send me further south after the Charleston assignment concluded, but the issue of the government car kept coming up. The car and I had to eventually get back home. I hung around to work a couple of airport sites and then headed back to DC in my car. When in DC, I also stayed at Doug's since Sampson and I had our own bedroom. I had no jealousy or concerns with their friendship or living arrangement, as I had gotten used to it long ago and it lessened my guilt. A week later, I was sent to San Juan, Puerto Rico, to serve as the lead advance agent for a Bernie Sanders visit. This was exactly what I was trying to avoid, but now I got the worst-case scenario: working as a lead agent in a place where my grasp of the language was conversational at best.

I knew I could handle the assignment, as I was a lead advance counterpart agent for a week in Haiti, when Former President Clinton visited there. I flew down with a ton of gear and settled in. The visit was to be a one- or two-night overnight visit, with multiple sites around the island. I had a few agents handling the various sites Sanders would visit, but they looked to me for decision-making. The supervisor on the ground was helpful. Whatever I couldn't resolve, I would kick it to him. I had to handle liaising with the Federal police and coordinating with the Clinton detail folks who were also visiting and happened to overlap Sanders' visit.

I worked from 7:00 AM to 11:00 PM every night that week, ensuring we had no gaps in our security plan. I put together the paperwork, got hotel rooms arranged for the arriving team, and kept the DC operations folks in the loop. Sanders arrived and the visit went smoothly. The lead agent is responsible for the majority of the work before the protectee sets foot on the ground. Once they arrive, your plan goes into effect. My stress level came down once things were in motion. There's no better feeling than when the event is over and the boss shakes your hand, saying you had done a good job. Though we had issues that week, mostly personality clashes, we pulled together and got the job done. Once I finished my duties, I headed to the water to swim for the first time in seven days on the island. My advance team was also exhausted; over drinks that evening, the twenty-year veteran agent told me he'd never before been so stressed in his career. I was proud of my team; it was a hellacious week, and I couldn't fathom spending an entire year being a lead agent. Fuck that mess.

As was becoming common, I returned home and was sent right back out on the road. But this time I had a team of Homeland Security Investigations (HSI) special agents assigned to me for the three-week rotation on the road and it would be how the rest of the campaign would go, just me and a team of HSI agents I didn't know.

During one of my three-week rotations back in DC, in early June 2016, Sampson and I closed on our new home in Virginia and moved in. The place was huge and made the furniture from our condo look like it was sitting in a doll house. We would need to invest in furniture for an office area, formal dining area, more living room furniture, and a nursery. The finishes were top notch: a huge walk-in shower with dual shower heads, stunning kitchen countertops and high-end appliances, lots of natural light from windows that overlooked the park, and dark cherry stairs that made the rooms pop. Our new home was the largest and nicest place I had ever lived in, as well as the largest mortgage payment I ever paid. But if it brought Sampson and I closer, I was fine with it. He was excited to decorate, pick paint colors for the walls, and plot out his vision for the place. He had a keen eye for interior design and seemed to make him happy. Unfortunately, the 4Runner that we'd purchased didn't fit the garage; it was like shoving a bear into a doghouse. I was approaching my permanent protective detail time and I would be driving the truck daily to and from work, so it made sense to downsize for gas mileage. Sampson suggested the Audi A3 e-tron as a replacement, and I liked the car. They were offering good lease deals on the car and our 4Runner somehow retained most of its value, despite it being slightly used, so we traded it in for the Audi.

On June 13, we awoke to hear of the shooting at the Pulse gay nightclub in Orlando, Florida. The death toll was 49 people, with 53 wounded. Mass shootings were becoming the norm in our society, but this broke my heart, happening to my own community. I texted friends who lived in the area to learn they were unharmed—but many had lost close friends. I had been to Pulse numerous times, so I knew where they had died, helpless and trapped, their lives ripped from them for no reason.

I was enraged, longing to help in any way possible. We donated to the Pulse fund, but it wasn't enough for me. I contacted the Human Rights Campaign and asked how I could effect change to ensure this doesn't happen again. They invited us to attend a meeting at HRC headquarters where we met really great people. They were seeking people to represent HRC in the Marine Corps Marathon that October, so I signed up to run with their team, Athletes for Equality. I'd have to raise $1,500, which would help reform gun laws, and all I had to do was run. I'd never run a race before, but I was prepared to run in memory of the Pulse victims.

On the campaign trail, we plugged along, city by city, state by state. My Dallas team was good company but skewed older. One of the agents on the team was an avid runner, so we made it a point to do runs together in Central Park or other cities and towns along the way. My San Juan/Miami team was fun. But the best was a visit to Provincetown, Massachusetts for a Hillary fundraiser starring Cher in August 2016. My team stayed on the Cape for a night before heading up to Ptown. Cher was one of those must-meet gay icons. I also had friends staying in Ptown for the summer. Carnival Week had just ended and the streets were still covered in glitter from the parade. It wasn't until we parked and got coffee that my San Juan based HSI team suddenly figured out they were surrounded by gays and I, myself, was gay. The look on their face was priceless. Cautiously, my shocked straight agents wandered off on their own. I met up for a while with friends – a rare experience during work.

Later, I headed for the venue for the event. The crowds were gathering. It was a great experience to represent the Secret Service as a gay man, while connecting with my community. I was near Cher but decided not to sacrifice my professionalism by greeting her. I merely watched in awe.

Soon after the event, a friend, Tom from Fort Lauderdale, alerted me to a Facebook post about the Cher fundraiser. His friend had snapped a photo of me, writing that it was about time they sent a Secret Service agent who fit in with Ptown. It was flattering.

Once back in DC, I was assigned to work the Vice-Presidential Debate, being held at Longwood University. I hadn't been back to Longwood since I left there in December 2003, for the Sheriff's Office. I was excited about going back as an agent. I would be handling all communications and radio traffic since I knew the campus layout better than my colleagues.

My favorite HSI team was a mix of agents from the west, Texas to Colorado. Unlike the other teams who usually came from the same field office, this team didn't really know each other. This forced us to socialize together. We had an absolute blast; whether it was working or playing pool after-hours, our new friendships were great. We teased one another but looked out for each other. I teased the two agents who continuously flirted with each other despite both having significant others at home, learned about bourbon from the Kentucky agent, and bonded with a gay agent who had assisted me in San Juan, Puerto Rico, months prior.

During this time, I was also training for the marathon. I would do one shorter run during the week and, as the training progressed, one long run that grew in distance. One of my favorite training runs was in Des Moines, Iowa, on the Clive Greenbelt Trail. It began in West Des Moines and ended up in Des Moines. I logged 19 miles on that path. The longest run was twenty miles, since that's what the training program called for. I had no issue with the long runs when it came to fitness or fatigue. When I signed up for the marathon, I had hoped Sampson would take interest in it as well and would be something we could do together, but he had no interest in accompanying me at all, via foot or bike, despite his lean figure that would accel at it. We both had gym memberships and as much as I loved working out, he never seemed to be into it as much as I was, and it wasn't something I could force him to do or enjoy more. The marathon training became just another adventure I would take on my own.

While I was home that fall, Sampson bought a new car for himself. He decided that once I was done with the campaign travels, we would only have the Audi between us. I wasn't thrilled with the purchase, but I didn't push back. We never did when it came to large purchases, a significant fault in our relationship. I remember thinking that the car was in his name alone and signaled he was becoming financially independent. We had slowly changed from lovers into roommates. I would come home after three weeks on the road, and be disappointed to be greeted without enthusiasm. Nothing he did suggested we were married. Though we still shared a bed and a home, the relationship felt more transactional than blissful. Even when we kissed, there was no passion or sense of connection. I wondered if this was how it was supposed to be or if this was how the rest of my life would be.

October approached and I was home for the three weeks during the marathon. On race day, I woke up at 4:00 AM to begin prepping. I donned a blue HRC equality logo tank top and I fabricated a Pulse Nightclub sign that would hang below my bib.

I had blindly placed myself in the 4 hour and 30-minute race group, uncertain what my pace would be. There were thousands of runners to contend with. My nerves were high, but the energy in my running group was invigorating. I was excited to be among a variety of people: twice my age, half my age, handicapped, ultra-marathoners, first timers.

The gun went off and, group by group, we set out for a lap around the DC area. I had my phone on my arm and Apple watch on. The cheers from the crowds were more than enough motivation to continue running. I hadn't experienced anything like it before. The military plays a large role in the marathon and manned most of the water stations. Mile after mile, as I passed, people would yell out "Go HRC", which made me smile and wave.

I spent most of the first half of the race running past people. Around mile eighteen, people were slowing and the crowd was thinning out, which allowed me to run at a faster pace. My pace improved at every passing 5k marker. I stopped at one of the HRC pit stops, where Sampson was assisting the HRC support group, for quick photos, and continued along. I felt great and was happy to see Sampson had made it to the checkpoint, I had been worried he wouldn't make it. I approached beer mile, where supporters line a section of the route and pass out a cup of beer to runners, and rewarded myself with some suds as I was nearing the finish.

There's a downhill run towards the finish line and I sped up heading down the hill, hoping to finish in under four hours. What I had forgotten about, however, was a steep incline at the Iwo Jima Memorial. I trudged up the hill and crossed the finish line at 4:03. I was thrilled. A few people thanked me for wearing the Pulse banner, which made it all worthwhile. I collected my medal and went to the nearest Metro stop, to meet Sampson to head home.

Sampson and I arranged to host a thank-you brunch following the race for those who had donated to my cause. Sampson loved to entertain and since our home was new, it was a chance to show off the new pad to neighbors and friends. I ended up raising far above the minimum for HRC, thanks to the generous donors.

The campaign sent me to Orlando the very next morning. I packed my bags, my marathon bib/Pulse banner, and a Marine Corps Marathon finisher patch and headed for Orlando. I knew I had to go to Pulse and pay my respects.

I had underestimated the feelings it would evoke, to be there in person, to see the makeshift memorial erected by mourners. I solemnly hung my bib, banner, and patch on the fence. About a month later, I received an email that a donation had been made to my HRC fundraising account. I was perplexed, given the race was long over. I tracked down the donor through social media and thanked him. He told me he'd seen my marathon stuff hanging on the Pulse fence, so he thanked me by donating.

The final month of the presidential campaign was a total blur. Hillary and Trump had begun doing more than one event per day, which meant we were leapfrogging all over the country and working back-to-back events. The Hillary events were fairly standard political rallies and I appreciated the normalcy that accompanied them. I preferred to work those venues since I knew what to expect. The Trump events, however, were usually chaotic. The atmosphere at those rallies were a mixture of a NASCAR race and a monster truck event. The crowds were huge and borderline fanatical, a clear sign of his popularity. The crowds were *very* white and I felt obligated to keep an eye on any minorities attending, fearing they'd be harmed by the mob. Large gatherings of likeminded people, mostly without college degrees, and loudly jingoistic, is a terrifying thing. There were seas of red MAGA hats and an abundance of camouflage clothing. But thankfully the crowds abided by agent rules.

On the eve of election day, my team ended up in Michigan for a Hillary event. Trump added a last-minute event in the same city: a midnight rally heading into Election Day. The turnout was shockingly large, and we ended up working a ridiculously long day. They came, they spoke, they left, and our job was done.

I called to get me and my team flights home on Election Day. I made it home by the afternoon and we invited friends over to watch the election results that evening. As millions of Americans watched, hour by hour, our reality and expectations were flipped upside down. The excitement I had experienced in 2012 wouldn't happen again. I truly didn't think those rally attendees would turn out to vote; but, like the polls, I was dead wrong. They loved the circus they had witnessed and wanted to throw a stick into the bicycle wheel that'd been overlooking them for years. Thanks to the Electoral College, they succeeded.

When I finally went to bed after midnight, I couldn't really sleep much. I was hoping the slow counts would turn the tide to Hillary's favor. I woke up to the jarring news that Trump would be the next President. There was a crestfallen mood and a disbelief in DC for months after, everyone in total shock. But I was grateful for the career decision I'd made months prior. Over the summer, my peers were asked to identify agents interested in forming the Obama Protective Division.

At the time, it was a total unknown who would win the election, but my options, as I saw them, weren't great. If Hillary were to win, I didn't think they would travel a lot and would remain in

DC, therefore making my work mundane. If Trump were to win, it would be a total wild card, given the size of his family and his rhetoric. Besides, I didn't want to partake in that. So I threw my name in the hat to go with Obama. Since their primary residence was in DC, I wouldn't travel as much. And they would surely travel to Hawaii often (one of my favorite places on earth). After a few years, I would be permitted to rotate off to the President's or Vice-President's detail. It seemed like a win.

Prior to Election Day, I was told I had gotten my wish. I would transfer to the Obama Protective Division, effective late November 2016.

CHAPTER TEN

O FFICIALLY, I BEGAN MY PROTECTIVE detail time, also known as phase two, with the Obama Protective Division (OPD) in late November 2016. In reality, I was still bouncing around the Washington Field Office, but as a member of OPD. There were myriad things to take care of when a new division is formed, and I was helping to get things up and running before the Obamas left the White House in late January 2017. It was a good opportunity to work with my new bosses and local agents, since we would be spending an asinine amount of time together over the next three to six years. I heard that agents leaving the field office would be working the Trump inauguration, a task packaged as a farewell gift from WFO management since we'd done so well in that office. Approximately zero of us viewed it as an honor, as a National Security Special Event venue is a massive pain in the ass to work.

I was assigned the formal ball on the eve of the inauguration at Union Station. The VIPs who would attend included the President-Elect, Vice-President-Elect, Cabinet members, military generals, and congressmen. The station, which offers train, subway, bus, and taxi services, would remain open during the event. This would be perhaps the most challenging site advance of my career.

After the usual meetings and multiple visits and walk-throughs with management, the President's detail site agent showed up. Due to the complexity of the venue, he decided to handle his protectee and I'd handle everything else. I had a new agent from WFO as my assist. Gameday arrived and the event transpired without any bumps. Walking into Union Station that night, you would have never known it from how it looked just a day prior. Elegant white curtains hung from the balconies, security measures hidden by blue drapes, and bouquets of red, white, and blue flowers sat atop of every table in the main hall. The VIPs moved effortlessly and safely through the station, unaware of how much work was involved to make it so. Exactly what we wanted. My assist was superb, handling minor issues that popped up outside of the venue. I was later told by senior management that my site was the most complex of the inauguration. I was pleased to know they recognized it.

The next morning, I reverted back to the Obama Protective Division. My assignment was to help get the armored limos out to Andrews Air Force Base, since Obama would depart following Trump's swearing-in. My new peers and I saw the swearing-in on TV, and then watched the Obamas board Marine One for the last time. It was surreal to watch. Once Marine One landed at the Air Force base, the Obamas and most of my colleagues boarded Air Force One, while I stood on the tarmac and watched them go wheels up, green with envy. But I had another assignment the next day: to protect one of the Obama daughters.

My first trip with the Obama Division was a good one; in late January, we traveled to the world-famous Sundance Film Festival and were surrounded by Hollywood actors. Standing backstage with award winning actors and viewing their movies prior to the public release was great. I had also never seen so much snow in my life, and I was thankful my driving experience in Pennsylvania winters had prepared me for the trip. It would set the tone for my time guarding the Obamas.

Once back from Park City, Utah, our teams were off to the British Virgin Islands (BVI) where the Obama family vacationed. Due to the housing on the British Virgin Islands, my team wasn't all in the same house, but my trio had the best accommodations. We had a private pool overlooking the breathtaking sound and nearby islands. I worked the morning shift to take full advantage of being in the tropics, watching yachts coming and going. Once our shift was over, we headed for the beach, hung out until the sunset with a Mai Tai, then ate dinner and retired. This routine was maintained for the entire trip. I had to pinch myself to ensure I was really getting paid to be in the tropics.

During one of the rare times I was home that winter, I was busy updating the adoption paperwork to reflect our new residence. It was complicated work, yet I was receiving zero help from my husband. I was feeling annoyed, so I raised the issue one night with Sampson as he was seated in the kitchen watching tv and I was combing through the paperwork on the counter. He paused and then told me he wasn't ready for kids. This was a momentous confession and an alarming one, given all the effort I had expended to get us to that point in the process. I immediately thought about the time and expense—approximately $15,000—involved in getting us approved for adoption. I thought of how other steps we had taken for the baby: a new home and a new car. For what?

I asked my husband when he would be ready for kids. He said he didn't know. I asked if he would ever be ready for kids. Again, he didn't know. I was upset, shocked, floored. I felt deceived, misled. I was at a loss for words as my thoughts raced. I couldn't force him to tell me anything he wasn't willing to admit, despite his folded arms and the appearance he had a whole lot more to say. I stood there dumbfounded and a moment later I walked out of the kitchen. Neither of us seemed to want to discuss it any further or admit our relationship was failing, so we didn't. I suddenly flashed back to our first break-up – remembering that it had been over our disagreement about children. What a fool I had been! Had Sampson been lying to me for a decade, only claiming he had changed his mind about adoption? Or was this decision new, given the deterioration of our relationship? Sampson and I hadn't been close of late, I was never home, and he was always alone. When I was home between trips, we sat in front of the massive new tv hanging on the wall binging Top Gear while also buried in our iPhones, rarely paying any real attention to each other.

That was the evening when I first began to emotionally withdraw from Sampson and our marriage. Instead of seeking counseling, it was how I reacted. As much as I prided myself on being a good communicator, I had failed where it mattered most. I did not stand up to him and our excesses. We lacked the balance that's required in relationships, where one partner can hold the other accountable, without fear of a massive fallout. Whether it was decisions about the endless car buying, moving, or buying nice watches, we were never able to keep each other in check when it was desperately needed. I went cold with him and though we were still sharing a home and bedroom, we had crossed into the roommate roles. I began volunteering for more overtime at work to avoid Sampson and the eventual conversation we would have to have. I didn't know what else to do. The adoption process was indefinitely on hold, similar to my feelings about our relationship.

When it came to traveling with the Obamas, I expected there would be movement in and around the DC area with sporadic trips to Hawaii. But I was way off. We were all over the globe! It made sense; they had been penned up in the White House under an insane amount of public scrutiny for eight long years, unable to make a move—or wear a tan suit—without being criticized. It was great to see them relax and enjoy themselves, for they'd surely earned it. Due to the level of work activity, I was unable to burn the vacation time that was accruing. But now that I had no marriage, where would I vacation—and with whom?

In April 2017, I took time off and went to Fort Lauderdale to unplug. Sampson was unable to go, as he was only receiving two weeks of vacation per year. But I was happy to be on my own. I had arrived at the start of Miami Beach Pride. So our old group of friends reserved hotel rooms in South Beach, to avoid the risk of a DUI. After day drinking, I went to my room for a disco nap and later met my friends at a rooftop party.

As I was chatting with a couple of my friends, a cute guy approached. My friends introduced me to Alex. He was confident but not arrogant. His black hair swept down to his brown eyes, but I mostly noticed his big smile. Alex, a Chinese American, was five feet eight inches tall, athletic build, and smooth skin. It was clear that I had a new preference in men. I bought Alex a drink and made small talk freely. It was obvious there was a connection beyond the physical attraction. He said he was planning to begin a PhD psych program in North Carolina that fall. I convinced him to accompany me to the dance party that evening.

We went down to my room so I could get cleaned up. We sat there a bit, gazing into each other's eyes. We headed down to meet the crew to walk to the club. Alex and I were already hand in hand. In fact, someone asked how long we had been together, assuming it had been a while. We posed for a group photo before entering the club and Alex leaned his head on my shoulder. The photo shows broad smiles on both of our faces.

It cost $60 apiece to enter the club, but we didn't even dance. We found a corner of the club, away from the others, and spent the entire evening in each other's laps, locked in a deep gaze. His smooth skin felt electric against mine. The music disappeared, the dancing boys faded into the background; the night belonged to us and we were the only two in it. It was an intensity I'd not known before, a complete and total freefall into Alex's being. I had to take deep breaths, as it was so intense. I couldn't put into words what was happening. Around 3:00 AM, Alex had to leave, and I felt an emptiness the moment he walked away.

We exchanged numbers and met up at Stork's coffee shop in Wilton Manors two days later. I wanted to verify if we still felt the same way we did on that special night. The more I learned about Alex, the stronger my feelings for him grew. He came from a modest family who taught him the value of education and hard work, passing on to him a drive for success and passion for life. He was 25, but mature well beyond his years.

I was still stuck with Sampson legally, and I admitted that to Alex. But that did not change his feelings; we were being pulled to one another by forces we couldn't fully control. The hours slipped by as we sat and talked. Before I knew it, I had to leave for dinner plans.

The next night, Alex came to my friends' house, where I was staying. My friends welcomed him with open arms and were very accommodating. After we all chatted a bit, they prepped the hot tub, laid towels out for us, and told us to enjoy the evening together. Perched on the Intercoastal Waterway, the home was dubbed "the glass house" and had water surrounding the backyard. The temperatures were perfect, and the moon was nearly full. Alex and I were in and out of the hot tub and ended up laying on a blanket underneath the stars where we talked for hours about life goals, aspirations, and relationship experiences and desires. We kept holding hands, caressing, occasionally making out. The same energy we had felt the first evening we met on the rooftop had only deepened. We must have stayed on the back lawn under the moon until 4:00 AM. We were getting tired but feared falling asleep, knowing we would have to part soon. It terrified me to know that I would have to say goodbye in the morning to this man who had changed my life. Alex was feeling the same way. We went into the guest bedroom and he fell asleep in my arms as the sun was coming up.

The morning arrived with a swift kick back to reality. I had to get to the airport and Alex had to get home. I packed up and we walked to the driveway. I felt this was the hardest goodbye I'd ever faced. Neither of us knew where to go from there, or when we would see each other again. The magnetic pull between us was so strong and our connection so surreal, I couldn't let this one walk away. I knew Alex was "the one." The fairytales you hear about, the love at first sight, the soulmate connection—all of that was here in front of me, embodied in one person.

I told Alex I would do whatever it took to be together again—including a divorce. We stood in the driveway, crying together, for the bond had been so great. We were afraid to say goodbye. As we embraced, I told him I loved him. Alex asked me to repeat it and I did. He repeated those very words back to me. Before I got in the car, he took the leather bracelet off of his wrist and placed it on mine, as a reminder until we were back in each other's arms. I drove away a total mess.

Once back home, I was acting strangely, given all I had just experienced. Though Sampson and I had an open relationship when it came to fooling around, I knew that falling for someone was a different ballgame—even though my days with Sampson were numbered. Sampson sensed that something was up. Eventually, I told him about this guy, saying we spent a lot of time together but there weren't any emotions involved. But the angst inside of me continued.

A week or so later while sitting in the kitchen watching tv, I confessed to Sampson that I had developed feelings for this unnamed guy in Florida. Sampson crossed his arms, and his face turned a shade of red, the way it did when his feelings had been hurt. He asked who it was, how serious it was, and what had occurred. I downplayed the situation, telling him things would be fine, but I needed some time to process everything that had happened. I had hurt Sampson and I felt guilty about it. Even though we weren't madly in love anymore, he was still my husband, a man I had spent a decade with, and I was now in unfamiliar waters having intense feelings for another man. Sampson didn't push back—not that he had an option to.

I continued my romantic contact with Alex, via text, FaceTime, and phone calls. I assured him that I planned to keep my promise about divorcing Sampson. I called Mom for advice, since she had been married a few times. She diplomatically didn't offer advice, but she empathized, agreeing that it sucks to lay down next to somebody that isn't your soulmate.

I began talking with my shift leader (a female agent who I had a great relationship with) and told her everything. I felt safe confiding in her, since she maintained utmost discretion and was free of judgement. She noticed the differences in my demeanor, how I talked about Sampson and how I talked about Alex, but said ultimately it would be my call on how to proceed.

Deep down, I feared carrying the label of a divorcee. My grandparents and siblings had all maintained their first marriages and I didn't want to be viewed as a failure. I realized that was my reason for staying with Sampson long after love had departed. I also realized I had clung to him because of my dream of parenthood, since all of my straight siblings had children and I wanted them as well. But now a future with Alex was all I could think about.

One night, about two weeks after meeting Alex, I decided it was time to come clean with Sampson, even if it meant flipping our lives upside down. Sampson was in bed watching TV, so I sat down and came clean. I wanted him to fully understand why I was doing what I was doing. I told him of the indescribable feelings, the soulmate connection, everything. I wanted to assure him Alex wasn't some "Miami fuck boy" as Sampson had called him after my initial confession. I insisted the whole thing wasn't Sampson's fault – but I was just being diplomatic. I had come to realize the major role he had played in our separation, notably his rejection of the adoption scenario.

Sampson was blindsided by what I told him. At least, his tears and words said so. But both of us knew this had not been working for a long time, even before Alex showed up. Still, I felt good that I was doing the right thing, and I knew I had to ask for a divorce.

The timing for a divorce is never great. But in this case, we had already planned a seven-day Caribbean cruise. It would mark Mom's sixtieth birthday and his father's retirement. We decided to proceed with the cruise. Meanwhile, I moved into our spare bedroom to begin the steps towards divorce. Luckily, I was traveling a lot in this period and was often out of the way. I vowed not to leave Sampson in a position where he couldn't provide for himself. We had separate accounts, but I held most of the joint funds in my account and immediately transferred his portion to his account. The home we were living in was enormous and neither of us wanted the burden of paying for it. It was decided we'd sell the home in the fall and go our separate ways.

We barely spoke following that major conversation. I don't know what he was thinking, but I was figuring out how to move forward to be with Alex. Sampson wasn't hateful towards me or throwing insults, but we avoided each other as much as we could. I joined the nearby LA Fitness so we could work out at different gyms and I often hung out at my shift leaders house on weekends, to avoid Sampson.

Days later, Sampson and I headed to Richmond to pick up his

Cory Allen

parents and drive to Cape Canaveral, Florida. We were to meet up with my mother and her husband, stay a night at my HSI friends' condo, and then head to the ship. Our parents had been made aware of our situation, making for an awkward drive to Florida with Sampson's parents and us in one car. Out of sheer habit, I held Sampson's hand during the drive south. He had been my partner and best friend for a long time. But meeting Alex had opened my eyes to the farce of my relationship with Sampson. There was no more ignoring reality.

The cruise went fine, even though we were forced to deal with each other for seven days in close quarters. We pushed our way through it, putting on a smile for most people. We never disrespected one another. We were hoping to salvage a friendship once the waters calmed. But we were honest with the other gays on the ship, who could sense something was going on between us. We saw no harm in being candid, and it helped to talk to others about our situation. I spent a lot of time using FaceTime, talking to Alex. Meanwhile, Sampson chose to deliver the news of the divorce to the world on Facebook.

Once we were back home, I traded in the Audi A3 to buy a 2017 Audi S3. Yet another kneejerk purchase. At work, I jumped on every trip I could, to minimize the awkwardness of living with your estranged spouse. A renowned Indian American neck and spine surgeon taught me how to ski while I was in the Rockies and I had a blast. That is, before dropping the N-word while on the slopes, thus ending our skiing relationship. I was bouncing all over the U.S., from LA to Florida to NYC.

My team took a long trip in June 2017 to the Tuscany region of Italy, where we were housed in a former church, circa 900 A.D.

177

One night, I was awakened by the sound of bottles being moving around the coffee table outside my bedroom. But when I peered around, no one was there. I decided the place was haunted, but when I asked the owners, they quickly changed the topic. We nicknamed the ghost Ethel and determined she came from the church graveyard. Ethel would knock on doors, open doors, and move stuff around the living room at night.

Next up was an Asia swing with the Obamas. I was the lead for my team for the trip and had the option to go to Hawaii and then jump early to Indonesia or remain in Hawaii for multiple days with no assignment before heading to Indonesia. I chose to hang out in Hawaii for a few days. We rented scooters and rode them around Oahu for a day. Hawaii has a small-town feel but is located in paradise. The gay community is close-knit, and it didn't take long to make friends there. The boys are beautiful, modest, and fun to be around. Alex and I continued our long-distance communications though we were cutting back on the frequency due to my ever-changing location and time zones. We didn't define or add a label to ourselves, since we were both dealing with significant life changes and were going with the flow of things.

After Hawaii, we continued to Yogyakarta, Indonesia. The city was utter chaos. Traffic was everywhere with no rhyme or reason as to the flow of it, with entire families stacked on scooters (no helmets). But it somehow worked. On one of our free mornings, we went to see ancient temples. Because we were obviously Americans, we were deemed very exotic and people asked to pose for photos with them. The crowd soon grew and began following us around. It escalated; people were now Facetiming loved ones and trying to get us in the frames. We eventually had to politely walk away.

Our group stayed at a high-end hotel that offered an amazing breakfast spread and massages for only $20. The hotel bartenders loved our large group, it was the only place we were allowed to have a drink and on our final night, the team gathered in the hotel bar. We managed to locate two microphones, connected them to the bar speakers, linked it with YouTube, and created our very own karaoke bar. After I had a couple of drinks, I took the stage and sang a number of country songs. It was a reminder of my early aspirations to be a professional singer. I still had it, I guess; everyone in the bar stopped what they were doing and listened to me. I had so much fun that night, revealing my hidden talents as a singer to my work family.

We left Indonesia and headed to South Korea for a few days. I set out to get a feel for the city. I met up with a Korean-American I'd met via Grindr for coffee and talked about the gay scene. Online, the Korean guys were very forward—but in person it was different. I went to a popular bar in Itaewon and I was the only white guy in the place. Not a single person approached me. I learned later that it's a cultural thing among Koreans to save face and not be seen fraternizing with a Westerner.

I waded deeper into the realities of divorce, hiring a divorce attorney, and getting the pre-settlement agreement filed with the court. Life was a chaotic balancing act, including my DC life, my live-in estranged husband, incessant work travels, and my desire to be with Alex. Things with Alex were getting complicated, He was playing the role of boyfriend, best friend, confidante, and psychiatrist all at the same time. It was getting to be a lot, as every call with him was emotionally exhausting. He wanted to ensure I was processing things well. I felt he was pushing me in ways I wasn't used to. I loved having his support, but I worried if he were getting too involved in the mental aspects of my divorce.

In July of 2017, I flew back to Fort Lauderdale for long weekend with Alex in an obscure resort so we could avoid running into anyone I knew. It was the first time I had seen him since we parted ways three months prior and I was very nervous, not knowing if the feelings would still be strong. Upon landing in Fort Lauderdale, I met Alex in the terminal. He was leaning against a pole in baggage claim in a tank top and white shorts. When I saw his smile, I knew the feelings were still there.

We had an amazing three days tucked away in our own paradise, without a soul knowing I was in town. We ordered room service most days, lounged by the pool, and floated in each other's arms. Alex educated me on his methodologies of skincare. My routine consisted of using a moisturizer and sunscreen but there was a whole other world to this regimen. We talked about our futures. He was set to move to North Carolina in August, and I was prepared to make trips to visit him there. He promised to visit DC when he wasn't swamped with schoolwork. We agreed to keep things loose until my divorce was finalized, and until we knew how the immediate future would play out. Alex said he was patient and appreciated my honesty. He also wanted to ensure he was in a good mental place when he began his PhD program.

I felt it was time to stop using Alex as my psychiatrist, for I feared I wouldn't process the emotional toll of a divorce if he were my crutch through it all. I began to cut back on what-all I would tell him, choosing to digest matters on my own. The following month he would start school in North Carolina. I was excited to have him within driving distance, but I didn't factor in the huge demands of his PhD program. When I took a road trip to see him after his move, Alex spent a lot of time studying while I was there.

By the end of the visit, we decided it were best to put the brakes on our relationship for the time being until I was fully through the divorce and he was in the swing of things with his PhD program. We decided we would cut back on the intensity and allow things to happen more fluidly. If we didn't pull back, both of us feared potential calamity, given the major obligations we were both juggling. I wanted to ensure he was free to make new friends and mingle with other gays so he would have a support network in his new town. The last thing I wanted to do was ruin the potential of a future with him. Alex and I never had intercourse together; we only ventured as far as oral fun. I lusted and really cared for him but wanted to wait until I was truly single to cross that final threshold with Alex.

In Virginia, the pre-settlement agreement had been filed with the court and Sampson and I were in our six-month waiting window, before the official divorce. We put the house on the market. Within a month, it was under contract with a settlement date in early October 2017. During those months, I continued to stay in the guest room on the rare occasion I was home, and we began the process of dividing or selling household goods. Given the house was large, it was easy to split things down the middle. That way, neither of us would spend a lot of money to establish a new home. It was amicable and it was fair.

When I was home, I would check in with Sampson occasionally

about our relationship. I discussed where we went wrong and what we would do differently. We both agreed the openness of our relationship contributed to the downfall, as well as my job traveling. It was unfair of me to expect him to be the primary caretaker if we adopted children. I hadn't ever thought of it that way and he was right. We resolved to remain friends when the dust settled, since we had spent eleven years together. We agreed that we were different people than when we first met – but we could not have reached this fork in the road without our relationship together.

CHAPTER ELEVEN

THERE WERE COUNTLESS TRIPS FOR the Obama team in 2017. Many to California, another to Spain, and one with the older Obama daughter heading to college, where I volunteered to do a two-week assignment in Boston. Early on in Boston, I matched with a guy named Ben on Tinder. Over dinner he told me he was a radiologist and I told him what I did for a living, which he found hard to believe. I admired his work ethic, drive, and intelligence, that he immigrated to the U.S. from Taiwan by himself, attended an Ivy league school, and was in his final year of residency in Boston. After dinner we went for cocktails, where I playfully tousled his hair and we talked about our families. I was moved to learn he had donated a kidney to his brother. I was flattered to be in this sweet and giving man's company, who I felt was far beyond my league.

Ben and I hung out ten times while I was in Boston. Towards the end of the trip, he invited me to Hawaii in October, as he had vacation time to burn. I was in the final stages of moving out of the house I shared with my estranged husband. Sampson had moved out the first of October. I was also focused on buying my own condo in Arlington, but agreed to add a week in Hawaii to the mix, since I was able to rearrange my work schedule.

The sale of the house with Sampson went smoothly, likewise the purchase of my new condo in Arlington. I bought it on a Friday, had painters, flooring guys, and movers arrive Saturday, and flew to Hawaii on Monday. Given the stressful and chaotic conditions that I kept getting myself into, I operated very well.

My contact with Alex had dropped off dramatically since we'd last seen each other two months prior; from hot and heavy to a month or more without a text. I felt he was living his new life and I was exploring mine. The week in Hawaii with Ben was perfection. We had a lot in common, as we went hiking, watched sunsets, had acai bowls for breakfast, toured the island in a rented Jeep, and hiked the Pillbox Hike overlooking Lanikai. We thoroughly enjoyed ourselves, sexually as well. At the end of the trip, I was wondering where we would go from here? During our last romantic dinner on the island, I asked Ben what he thought of our situation. His response was, Well, you haven't asked me to be your boyfriend. So I asked and he agreed Admittedly, I felt under pressure at that moment but I began planning another two-week Boston assignment so we could spend more time together.

I'm not sure why I felt pressured to formalize our relationship, but felt Ben was such a catch—so what could go wrong? (By now, readers might see a familiar dating pattern.) When I got home and told my friends my dating news over photos from Hawaii, they were quietly skeptical. But that didn't register with me. I was proud to say I had a new boyfriend and explained that I would time my housewarming party with his DC visit. I was eager to introduce him to everyone. In hindsight, I realize showing off Ben like a new sports car from a midlife crisis was my attempt to show everyone I was okay post-Sampson and moving on.

On my next two-week Boston swing, Ben and I picked up where we left off. We spent every day together, before and after work. I'd walk him to or from the hospital and we would spend the night with each other, rotating from his place in Back Bay to my hotel near Fenway Park. We visited Boston museums, went shopping, went out to eat, made dinner at his place, and binged *Stranger Things on* Netflix. I enjoyed his company a lot.

Around this time, I had decided it was time to go back to school and obtain a Master's Degree. It was something I had always wanted to do, since a Bachelor's Degree doesn't do much to set one apart anymore. I wanted to set the bar high for my future children as well as feel a little more accomplished, given the doctor I was now dating. I found the Master of Public Administration program at George Mason University was renowned, close by, and didn't require GRE scores. It had been a decade since I had taken classes, so I had to ask Secret Service bosses for letters of recommendations. I wrote an essay about my desires to make changes in the criminal justice system, focusing on racial disparities, and LGBTQ communities in particular. In November 2017, I was accepted into the Spring 2018 program at the Schar School of Government at George Mason. I was really proud of myself. Since the rupture with Sampson, I was seeking changes on all fronts. I also craved a new challenge, as I was not good with being idle, mentally or physically. I felt attending grad school would provide a new sense of normalcy and would help better myself. My bosses affirmed they would support me in my educational endeavors, since the classes were in person and mostly on the Arlington, VA campus.

I made another trip to Boston a week before Christmas 2017 for a long weekend with Ben. It would be two months before we'd see each other again, due to Obama work that would take me to Hawaii for Christmas and the New Year, and Ben's travel plans. I stayed at his place and found myself cleaning it while he was at work. The kitchen was usually a mess: dishes stacked in the sink, cabinets ajar, cups everywhere, so this was my primary focus. I realized my level of OCD was off the charts and I was forgetting it wasn't my home. I suddenly started to picture myself as the husband who would forever be cleaning, since Ben worked long hours and was more casual about housekeeping. One morning as Ben headed out for work, he asked if I would do his laundry. I didn't mind since he was working, but I got spooked that a precedent was being set. I wondered if I was ready to embrace the role of the housewife to a doctor and be the lesser earning spouse, both of which were wild and unrealistic thoughts to be having.

Before leaving Boston for Hawaii for the holidays, I shopped for a few things for Ben's Christmas gifts. After he opened the gifts, including a new Fitbit and fancy chocolates, he looked at me gratefully and told me that he loved me. I was unprepared for this declaration. I mouthed the same words, but they did not come easily. I immediately knew I wasn't ready for it. Our relationship had taken a very serious turn in only three months and my gut was uneasy about it. As I left his place and headed for the airport, I knew I was in too deep. Ben had done nothing wrong at all. But my divorce wasn't finalized yet and in no way had I reconciled everything that was transpiring in my life, I never sat still long enough for things to sink in.

Upon arriving in Hawaii, Ben and I FaceTimed. I abruptly asked if we could back things up a bit. This didn't go over well; he felt rejected. Ben didn't know how else to take "backing things up" other than I was breaking up with him. We cried over FaceTime as I tried to explain why it made sense to slow things down.

The rest of the Hawaii trip was a train wreck, given my depression over Ben and everything else swirling around in my head. I tried to override my feelings; I went out galivanting the island, catching up with Hawaii friends, karaoke at Wang Chung's, afternoons on the beach, and generally concealing my emotions by never sitting still.

Once back in DC in January 2018, it was time to settle into my first semester as a graduate student. I hadn't a clue what to expect, since it had been a decade since I hit the books, but I was excited to be back in the classroom. The professor was younger than me and on top of her game when it came to public administration. In the first class, our syllabus confirmed that a ton of reading and writing was involved. I wasn't as mentally prepared for this as I had thought, but was determined to aggressively tackle the assignments and focus on the research paper, so I could prevent an end-of-the-semester meltdown.

In late January, I met Colin in DC, via Grindr, and we began to hang out on the weekends. He was from Hawaii, where we'd both just been a few weeks prior and we had friends in common. He had a bubbly personality, muscular legs, a great ass, and had an expansive friend network that he wasn't shy about introducing me to. He worked for one of the big four accounting firms and that consumed most of his life. Our dates consisted of hanging out at coffee shops while he did paperwork, and I did grad school stuff. He was into two-step and West Coast swing, which I began attending with him when work permitted. Colin was the first local guy I saw potential in, and I felt that DC might hold some promise regarding dating. He also was a way for me to avoid mentally processing everything I had been running from, though I didn't know it at the time. He was into cycling and talked a lot about the AIDS/Lifecycle Ride that goes from San Francisco to Los Angeles, raising money for the AIDS foundations in each city. I had been seeking an athletic outlet and was interested. Endurance was never an issue for me, so I didn't think training for the 545-mile bike ride would be too bad. In late February, after meeting members of Colin's cycling team at Number 9 (a DC gay bar), I decided to join the ride. No alarms went off inside about adding endurance training into the mix of attending grad school and working and traveling full-time. The ride wasn't until early June and I convinced myself that I could juggle everything.

After formally signing up for the ride with Colin's team, via invite, mostly composed of his co-workers, and ordering a Trek Domane SL8 Disc cycle, he suddenly freaked out and asked that I not ride with his team. He claimed he didn't want to mix his professional life with his personal life. I was pissed I'd done all this work thus far, only to be kicked off his team. I was determined to still do the ride and find a new team. But I still met up with his colleagues for weekend rides anyway.

We continued to date. Colin stayed at my condo every weekend. A month later, one night after dancing lessons, we went for ramen. This had been a typical twelve-hour day together, a long training ride, lunch, dinner, dancing, and late-night snack. When I was about done with my ramen, he announced that the relationship was over. He was afraid that I was falling for him and this was how he chose to handle it. I was legitimately hurt. I took an Uber home and that was the end of it for us. It was ironic that I had been treated just how I had treated Ben a few months prior. Life's odd like that, but it was a valuable lesson. The incident inspired me to reach out to Ben and apologize for how I had handled things with him.

As the school semester progressed, work was not holding up their end of the bargain. They were not supporting my academic career. I had been sent on the road unexpectedly several times, forcing me to miss classes. Given that the school had a limit regarding how many classes you can miss before you fail, this was concerning. My professor had worked with law enforcement, so she was understanding. I was turning in my assignments early, but if I failed the class due to attendance, I would be kicked out of the entire program for not maintaining a B average.

A business trip to Mexico was required in April 2018. Upper management promised I would be back in DC in time to attend class on Monday. But the trip was suddenly extended. I would miss my class, guaranteeing a failing grade. I was livid. To offset the stress, I went to the resort gym and climbed on a bike to aggressively spin for over an hour. I was so pissed off, I posted an angry rant on Facebook about my situation. By the end, there was a pool of sweat under the bike.

This was my breaking point. I had enough of this Secret Service lifestyle. I had given my all for years. But it didn't really matter. I was a cog in the wheel and was easily replaced. While I was grateful for everything I'd experienced, it was time for me to go. I had to take ownership of my life. We were all thankful for the unlimited overtime and amazing travel, but it comes at a high cost to your psyche and loved ones. You get burnt out. After a while, you don't care about the money or travel; you just want normalcy.

Way back in 2014, I'd begun seeking a work schedule that was strictly Monday through Friday. I had applied to dozens of other criminal investigator positions in the DC area, but the competition was so fierce, I couldn't even land an interview.

I knew I needed to reestablish myself, to find a loving man to build a family with, to be present in my own life. Now I had the resolve to make it happen. At the time, I was one of eight agents remaining from my academy graduation, out of twenty-three. That's not a very good retention rate. The survivors had an ongoing bet as to who would be the next to go. We also retained an ongoing fear that the longer we were in the protection phase of our career, the more separated we would become from conducting actual investigations. This becomes problematic when you land an interview with another agency and your last criminal investigation was several years ago. Your skillset diminishes and you become less relevant as an investigator. A friend of mine was at the four-year mark in his protective detail time and he had been passed over by a potential employer for that very reason. I feared getting to that point; I felt I had to act quickly to ensure my investigative experience was still relevant, or risk being left behind in my career.

After my rage abated, I emailed my DC professor. Thankfully, she was sensitive to my situation and agreed to not fail me.

Once back home, I had to buckle down for the AIDS/Lifecycle Ride. I'd done multiple long rides but hadn't surpassed the 75-mile mark yet. I would have to train for a one-hundred-mile ride but I was fully confident could accomplish it. It was a matter of finding the time to get it done. My days off were random and rotated so I ended up doing most of my training rides solo in the middle of the week. Friends of mine in San Francisco invited me to join Team Gilead, representing the company that created the highly profitable PrEP drugs. There was a $3,000 fundraising minimum for the ride, so I reached out to friends, colleagues, loved ones. By late April, I had raised nearly $5,000, with the average donation of $200. People left me speechless with their generosity.

On a Wednesday morning in late April, I set out for a practice seventy-five-mile ride, beginning on the Mt. Vernon Trail fifteen miles away from my condo. I figured I'd do the route twice, with added distance at the end. My bike had a computer to track my mileage, pace, cadence, and GPS routes. Around mile twenty-eight, I came upon a curve in a paved trail. Just then, the front wheel went off of the trail and I hit the pavement. I felt a familiar sensation in my hand and knew I had broken a bone.

I quickly jumped back on my feet to save face. I noticed a finger that was perpendicular to the others, numerous road rashes and bloody areas from my knee to my shoulder. My jersey kit was ripped in several locations. But the bike was fine. Thankfully, I was only two miles from home, so I called for an Uber XL. I got home, jumped in the shower, and then drove myself to the ER. They splinted my busted hand and referred me to an orthopedic surgeon.

A few days later, the surgeon provided me with two options. Either they set the finger in a cast and hope it heals correctly, or I get surgery to place pins in my hand, ensuring a full recovery. I opted for surgery, since finger dexterity is important in my career. The surgeon flatly told me I would not be able to do the AIDS/Lifecycle Ride. He warned that another crash would risk my losing the finger altogether. I sadly informed my teammates I would not be riding. This sense of defeat was not something I was used to. I had already raised close to $5,000, had my vacation approved and flights booked, so I decided to volunteer for the ride. I was on the advance route marking team, where we would place signage in advance for cyclists, every turn of the 545 miles, from San Francisco to Los Angeles. Given the advance work I'd done for the Secret Service, this role was a perfect fit. I'd get to travel through California for seven days in a vehicle with air conditioning.

While I had a partial cast on my left hand, I was able to perform my duties as an agent. During one assignment in Los Angeles, actor Tom Hanks noticed my hand. He asked if there was a cool story to accompany my cast, something along the lines of roughing someone up. I just laughed and said there wasn't. I was embarrassed he had noticed.

The spring semester quickly came to a close and I turned in my research paper on the effectiveness of crises intervention teams within police departments. The workload itself had been manageable, but I found that formatting and properly citing research were a pain in the ass. There is no handholding in grad school, either; it was all on me to figure it out. I ended up with an A+ in the course and I began to prep for the next class, statistics.

I recognized I was running my life at a pace that wasn't sustainable, but it was becoming clear that I didn't know how to sit still and enjoy my downtime at home. My mind was always focused on the next task, the next trip, the next adventure—and I didn't know how to slow it down. When I was in DC, I made certain to have lunches, dinners, and happy hours with close friends like Keith, David, and Tony, because I feared being left behind since I was never home. But my friends knew me best, understood the demands of my job, and were my sounding board for my dating life. I valued their input and, honestly, I needed it. Though they often ridiculed me for my frequent dating dilemmas, they kept me grounded. I loved them dearly.

Due to my bachelor status, I agreed to join Tony and a few other friends in Vegas for Matinee over Memorial Day weekend. It worked, since I would be traveling out to California for the AIDS/Lifecycle Ride a week later. I flew to Vegas with Tony and spent the next four days soaking up the sun, pool parties, dance parties, and the eye candy of gays in swimwear. I loved watching the parade of cute boys who would swim by and flash a coy smile as I lounged all day on a float in the pool.

I next flew from Vegas to San Francisco, where I spent a few days hanging out before beginning my Lifecycle volunteer work. I connected with other members of my advance team at the Cow Palace for orientation. We learned the final fundraising total was over sixteen million dollars. Everyone was super-nice, directing me like the lost child I was. Four of us would mark the entire 545-mile route: an older woman, an older transgendered man, a younger woman, and me. We were split into two teams of two. The younger girl, Suzie, and I paired up. The next morning, we began marking the route. Suzie preferred me to drive since I had vast experience dealing with traffic. I'd pull up to an intersection, park and shield Suzie with the car while she hung the signs. We made our way down the coast that way. We were spending up to fourteen hours a day in a car. I was in awe at the beauty of California. I made a decision that I'd one day live there. The week flew by. On the final day, we had to mark the final leg into downtown Los Angeles, where the cyclists would cross the finish line. Suzie and I both had red-eye flights home that day, so neither would see the cyclists arrive. We were later told the route we marked was the best they'd ever seen and invited to do it again the following year.

CHAPTER TWELVE

As soon as I arrived home in DC, I had to return for work to California in mid-June 2018. I escorted one of the Obamas through a shop in Beverly Hills, later that evening, I was on Tinder that visit and matched with a local guy. We met the next night for dinner in Beverly Hills. Joe was boyishly cute, well dressed, had an adorable laugh, and was a dog dad. As we talked, it became clear that he worked in the store we had visited the day before. But we hadn't seen each other despite me walking by him, for I was focused on doing my job and his eyes were glued to the protectee. We hit it off and had numerous dates that week. I would meet him in Beverly Hills for his lunch break. After work, we would have dinner together and then lounge at my hotel or his condo with his dog Louie. Joe was ten years younger than me and stood five foot six inches tall with an athletic build. He had great taste in music, fashion, and we had fantastic sex, and I told myself he had his act together, owning his condo, great career, and a being a good dog dad. At the end of my visit, we decided to have him fly to DC a month later. He told me that he admired my decisiveness and I soaked up his compliments, I liked him and wanted to get to know he and Louie more. Upon my departure, he gave me a card, thanking me for an amazing week. It included a line from a George Strait song and a hand drawn picture of two stick men and a dog. That impressed me. I told my friends about him and they gave me the skeptical eye that I expected from them.

Two days after I landed in DC, I was off to Europe. The first stop was Madrid. I had only been to Mallorca in the past and this was my first visit to mainland Spain. It was Pride weekend in Madrid that week and the city was adorned with rainbows, from city hall to the vibrant Chueca neighborhood. I had already plotted out my Pride events itinerary for the trip. Upon arriving, I dropped my bags, changed clothes, and headed out into the city to sightsee and find food. It was a great feeling to be in Madrid during the Pride celebration. I felt accepted.

My team colleagues were champs about everything and not once did they say anything derogative about the influx of gays in the city. The two agents I was closest with, my shift leader and Sal, were always the most supportive of me. They would happily accompany me anywhere I wanted, as the most genuine and accepting of the team. Due to the Obamas' itinerary, I had some time to enjoy the city before work began. I went to dinner with a large group of my peers and learned that Spaniards eat really late and don't even drink until midnight. After dinner, I headed downtown solo for a Pride dance party. I dropped a pin in an iMessage to my team peers and told them I would advise when I arrived back to the hotel, so they wouldn't worry. I could tell the boss was uneasy with the situation, but I manage myself well. The party was in a large venue along the waterfront. There were three levels to the place. I was early to the party, by European standards, and I made my way to the bar. The sound system, lights, screens, and stage were perfect. A crowd soon filled the place. I met some Londoners and hung out with them for the rest of the night, talking and dancing. The last night in Madrid, I attended a huge Pride street festival in the city center, attracting an estimated one million people. Merchants wandered through the crowds, selling beer for a euro. There were great bands and singers on stage all night.

I wandered from the city center into the Chueca neighborhood, making new friends. We wandered from bar to bar. A few of the guys in the group wanted to go to a bathhouse in Chueca and I agreed to go with them. My experience with bathhouses was limited to the one experience I had in DC, in 2009, but in Europe, they're far more common and normalized. The line to get in was long but we waited. Once we got in, one of the guys, a tall twenty-something Spaniard with juicy lips, found an empty room and pulled me into it, where we hooked up. I figured this was a once-in-a- lifetime experience, SO why not enjoy it. When we left the bathhouse a couple of hours later, the queue was wrapped completely around the block. There were people still drinking, dancing and singing in the streets, as the sun was coming up. As I walked into the hotel I ran into my team, eating breakfast. I saw the grins spread across their faces, but I didn't care; Madrid was totally worth it.

The next stop was Paris. I adore that city. Again, I was able to have a free day to enjoy the city. The trip coincided with Bastille Day and the World Cup, making for a very unique vibe to the city. The hotel concierge arranged tickets for us to see the Louvre and the Catacombs. Though macabre, the Catacombs were pretty badass. Millions of Parisians moved and meticulously stacked in one location, centuries ago.

That night, two of my single peers and I took a cab to the Fireman's Ball, a large celebration coinciding with Bastille Day, where Parisian fire stations open their red doors to the public and host an all-night party to raise money for the fire station. We were in a long queue when the crowd, thousands of people, drinking heavily, began shoving forward. I didn't get a comfortable feeling, so I left my coworkers.

I love that exciting feeling in my stomach, when I walk solo into a club and know the world is my oyster to make the night whatever I want it to be. I felt that sensation again that night in Paris. There's something liberating about wandering a city, experiencing new gay bars, and seeing everyday life in other cultures. I headed for Le Marais, the gay neighborhood, where I chose to watch the shower show at Raidd Bar before wandering to other bars. I had my gay apps on and was chatting with a guy who was nearby and visiting from Australia. We met up, he was great to talk to, and we decided to bar-hop together for the rest of the night.

I was on midnight shift and I working twelve-hour shifts in Paris. Work would occupy the rest of my time in country, but I didn't mind. One of the nights involved the final game of the World Cup, which was being broadcast in the stadium prior to the concert by Beyoncé and Jay-Z. I was onstage and watching the huge monitor as France won the world cup. The stadium erupted in cheers and celebrations, and thousands of French flags were being waved. It was a historic moment. The concert was amazing. During the show, I thought to myself, I'm getting paid to stand here in Paris as

Beyoncé and Jay-Z do their thing a few feet away from me.

After the Europe trip, Joe (the Beverly Hills retail guy) came to visit me in DC and I had a good time showing him the DC area. We toured Mount Vernon and the monuments around DC, and visited the Smithsonian museums. By the end of his visit, we resolved to continue getting to know one another, despite living on opposite coasts. We had mutual interests: we both desired a family, loved dogs, travel, family, nice cars, and he was dropping hints that he desired a relationship. Since I was often in California for work and rarely at home, attempting to date someone long-distance didn't seem a stretch. On the work side, I had made my interest known that I wanted to come off of the traveling shift and move into our operations. The operations role would provide stability and that would help with my school schedule, and allow me to be home more. I would enjoy a year of work consistency before my transfer to the President or Vice-President's detail and could travel to see Joe on our own schedule. Operations is a sought-after position on a protective detail or in a field office, as it is the epicenter for information. These agents work behind the scenes to ensure the working and traveling shifts have what they need to fulfill the mission. Without Operations, the details would not be able to function. For an agent like me, worried about my skillset diminishing on a protective detail, this was a good way to distinguish myself from my peers.

I made additional trips to the LA area for work in August, bookended with a few days off to stay with Joe. One two occasions, Joe told me he had planned a weekend getaway for us but he refused to tell me where we were headed. The first trip took us to Laguna

Beach, where he had booked us a suite at the Montage Laguna Beach. I was in awe at its beauty. Our hotel room overlooked the picturesque beach, and we spent the weekend taking in the views. We walked the beach together nervously talking around the state of our relationship. I wondered who this man was, that was going to such an extent to impress me. Was he too good to be true? I asked him if he would want to make things official. He excitedly said yes. I felt comfortable in my own skin with him. I could belt out Blake Shelton songs in the car with him or indulge in sugary baked goods together.

A couple of weeks later on my next visit, Joe, dressed more casually in a tee shirt and slim fitting jeans, surprised me with a weekend at the Ojai Valley Inn, another five-star resort where I had coincidentally been a few weeks prior due to work. I hadn't had someone treat me so well before; it felt odd to be showered with gifts and trips. I assured Joe I didn't need five-star resort weekends or Prada wallets to be happy or be impressed by him. I only needed his company. We had his dog Louie with us, who I was also growing to adore, and on one of the nights around the firepit, we met two women who were SiriusXM radio hosts for a relationship advice channel. They loved our story, as short as it was, and encouraged us to keep in touch with them, on the radio or via Instagram.

On our final night in Ojai, we laid out under the stars and gazed upwards, both happy we were officially boyfriends and both happy with where things were headed. Once I returned home from the trip, I learned I would rotate into the Operations section, effective September 2018, where I would once again be working with my warm female team leader, who had moved there a few months prior.

The downside was that I had been selected to be the lead advance agent for a trip to Finland that same month. Combined with another trip, it meant I would miss the first three weeks of grad school that semester. I made the difficult decision to put off school, since turning down assignments would've reflected poorly on me. I would eventually learn the extensive demands on an agent in Operations, meaning I made the right decision in taking the semester off. The Finland trip would be my first foreign lead advance since my work for Bernie Sanders in Puerto Rico during the 2016 campaign. But this looked to be much smoother, based on who was assigned to my team and the short duration of the visit. I had not been to the Nordic region before and it didn't let me down. My cousin had lived in Helsinki for two years and was helpful in suggesting where to go. The city was very clean, and people were friendly, though most of the men were blonds with blue eyes and long names that began with a J. As the lead, I had the bulk of the work, but the hotel had a lounge where I did the majority of my paperwork while looking out at the river. The two agents assisting me had a considerable amount of time on the job. The visit went very well.

I had applied for a position within an Office of Inspector General in Fresno, California, sometime in August. It was a gamble, since the salary was two pay grades below my own. But it was located in Fresno, meaning I would be closer to Joe, who lived in Los Angeles. Once home from Finland, I received a call from the supervisor of the Fresno OIG office, asking for an interview. It wasn't feasible to fly to Fresno on short notice without it costing a fortune, so we planned a phone panel interview. I had not done a phone interview before, and I immediately didn't like it. I usually read people's body language really well and adjust my responses to them for maximum effect. This time, I had no visual cues.

I had no idea as to the level of stress Operations presented, but it had to be handled. I'd have to respond to one hundred emails a day. Protection is a fluid animal and requires 24/7 attention when something comes up. My work phone was with me at all times and I was incessantly checking it to ensure things on the detail were operating smoothly. Someone calls out sick an hour before their shift, they call Ops to find someone for a replacement. Flights get delayed, call Ops. Rental car or hotel not accurate, call Ops. Someone thinks they've been screwed out of an hour of overtime, call Ops. Need to know what trips are in queue, call Ops. People easily forgot how often they'd get the proverbial bear (coming out ahead in work hours), but the moment they had to sacrifice ten extra minutes of their time, they call Ops and complain. The bosses knew they could call us at any hour, and we would know what was going on and what assets were in what locations. This was my life as an Ops agent. Though I often cursed it, I also loved it.

I loved having a normal schedule, although my off-duty time was gobbled up by incessant questions via cell phone. I was home on a regular basis. Joe and I were dating that fall. He was busy at the LVMH luxury brand, overseeing multiple accounts in Los Angeles. But his job abruptly ended—with only two days' notice for him and other account managers. This was a setback, but it allowed Joe to join me in Palm Springs, the luxurious gay destination, for a weekend.

While we were hanging out one day, Joe received a text message that I happened to see. The message was "send nudes?" When I asked him about it, he said it was a former coworker who was being goofy and "nudes" is also used interchangeably with noodles. I let that slide, because I still hadn't learned about recognizing red flags.

Since I had a more predictable and consistent schedule, I decided to adopt a puppy. The shelters were full of larger dogs and mostly Pit-Bull mixes, which did not fit my lifestyle. A friend of mine had a Sheltie. I liked the demeanor of his dog, so I found a breeder in Maryland and brought home Simba. I was once again a dog daddy. I had forgotten how much work a puppy is, but my condo had hardwood floors and tile in the bathroom, proving to be very helpful when your puppy isn't yet housebroken and walks fifteen yards while peeing.

Simba had a sweet disposition and was fluffy and inquisitive. He never whined or cried and immediately had an obsession for balls and a favorite stuffed squirrel. He was quick to learn and not stubborn like my cherished Jack Russell had been, though Simba was timid. Raising your voice or even looking at him differently would make him cower. He only wanted to please me and listened very well.

December rolled around and I was prepping for another traditional Christmas and New Year in Hawaii. On the morning of December 11, an email informed me that I had not been selected for the OIG position in Fresno. I'd assumed as much, since months had passed without feedback on the panel interview. A few hours later, however, my cellphone rang—and the caller ID was Fresno! It was the supervisor of the OIG office, asking if I was still interested in working there. They had filled the original position, but an agent had just given his two weeks' notice to transfer to another federal agency. The vacated position was at my current pay grade. I knew I had to accept the position, even if it meant moving my life to California. This was my chance to break free, to take ownership of my life, to seek the things I desired most. I set up another interview with the agent in charge of the West Coast division, to get his blessing on the hire.

A week later, I met with the Special Agent in Charge. I told him all about myself. I talked about things I'd studied up on, like Congressional reports, their five-year plan, recent cases of interest. I even mentioned that I was dating someone who lived in LA. I felt I'd nailed the interview. He told me he can move agents around his division. While Fresno isn't ideal, he admitted, they'll get me where I wanted to go in due time. By day's end, he offered me the position, which I accepted.

Now that I had the final verbal offer, it was time to tell the agents in Ops as well as the bosses. I had a fear of repercussions, but hoped I wouldn't be punished by peers for seeking a better life for myself. I felt I had to make my case to everyone, to avoid the appearance of quitting the team. Several bosses congratulated me and said they wished they'd done the same years ago. My former shift leader and now the agent in charge of Operations was very supportive, as she'd always been regarding anything I aspired to. She fully understood the sacrifices one must make for the job and by this point in her career, she would not be having children herself. I knew I would miss her leadership, her support, and her shoulder. I thought back to all of the advice sessions about life changes and boy dramas I had demanded of her.

I made another trip to LA to see Joe, prior to leaving for Hawaii for Christmas. Joe had been seeking out employment and taking stock of his life as well. I delivered my career news. In response, he suggested moving to Fresno with me, but I pushed back. I didn't want him to be a glorified houseboy to me, since he was unemployed, and the Fresno job market offered few opportunities. He had a job lead in New York City, but decided to stay in Los Angeles since I would be moving to Fresno. Joe was fine with weekends together until I got transferred closer to him. On numerous occasions, he'd half-jokingly say things like "When are you going to marry me?" There was no further evidence of sexting or other foolishness, so I trusted him and wanted to continue to build upon what we already had. Things were looking up on all accounts.

Two days before I flew to Hawaii, Joe called me with unexpected news: He accepted the position in New York City, and would be moving in January. I was stupefied; it went against everything he had just told me in person, repeatedly, about building a relationship with me on the West Coast. Now that I was moving closer to him, he was relocating to the other side of the country. We were back to a long-distance relationship. I was confused and hurt.

We talked via FaceTime and I asked for a few days to gather my thoughts on our situation. I needed to ask myself what was going on, and whether I could handle an extended long-distance relationship. I didn't understand what Joe's priorities were. I tried to tell him the salary he was being offered was not going to go very far living in Manhattan, once rent and taxes were factored in, but he wouldn't hear it.

A few days later, I called things off with Joe on FaceTime. It was apparent his focus was going to be on his career. I didn't fault him for it, but he had previously made me believe he truly wanted a serious relationship, and now his actions spoke otherwise. I loved him, but it was time to focus on my new life in a new state. Joe said he understood, he was excited for his move to NYC and now without Joe in Los Angeles, I wasn't as excited about Fresno but still knew it was what I had to do.

Days later, I headed to Hawaii for my last work trip. The Trump government shutdown over the budget impasse was in full effect at this time, meaning my pay was frozen. Luckily, I had taken a travel advance. Hawaii was fantastic as always. I was working the evening shift, as one of Michelle Obama's security agents, so I could sleep in the mornings and then be out socializing after work. News of my new job spread like wildfire among fellow agents. Everyone was supportive.

My life, I had belated realized, was more than the badge I wore on my belt. But I had seen this mindset in co-workers over the years. Guys hustle for the overtime, the promotion, the prestige. They lose multiple spouses to the demands of the job. Thus, at retirement, they have no family to enrich their lives. I vowed that would not be me.

On one of my final nights in Hawaii, I was alone with my thoughts and staring out into the darkness of the Kailua waters. I was thinking about my career and the next adventure. As I let my mind wander, something in the water kept catching my eye. But nothing appeared when I put on my night vision goggles. It got bright enough that I realized it was bioluminescence waves as they crested. The seductive phenomenon offered a memorable finale to my final trip to Hawaii with the Secret Service.

The government shutdown lasted far longer than any of us thought: thirty-five days. It put the brakes on my transfer and relocation. My new boss assured me the position would still be mine. But I HAD learned that until things are in writing, there's no guarantee. My Secret Service bosses allowed me to stay in Operations, since we didn't know when I would be moving. My condo in Arlington, VA was also in limbo. I had a management company on standby ready to locate a tenant for me, but it all relied on when the government reopened. When it did finally reopen, over a month later, there was an aggravating delay in my transfer. I set a tentative transfer date in early April, hoping for the best.

During all of this, I made a couple of trips to New York City to see Joe. We never ceased texting each other since we had officially broken up. I understood why he took the job in New York City, after all, I was ten years ahead of him in life and in my career and I couldn't fault him for his decision. I wanted him to be successful and happy in his career. We were comparing notes, costs, moving information. I had held out hope that we could see things through, since I loved him.

On my first visit to NYC, I was there when his movers arrived and helped get his Manhattan studio unpacked. We talked at length about his career, my impending new job in Fresno, and why he made the decision to move across the country. He assured me he was only going to be in NYC for one year and then he would transfer back to LA or San Francisco, where he was originally from and still had family. He told me he was dead-set on the one-year timeline and asked I keep him on it, no matter what. He said he wanted the experience of opening a Louve store on Fifth Avenue and that would be a springboard for his future. He was adamant on having a family and would focus on that goal after his year in NYC was up. These words resonated with me, since I was seeking the same things and had seen how loving, gentle, and caring he could be.

I decided I wasn't mad at Joe for taking the job in NYC, as I would never fault someone for bettering themselves, personally or professionally. I asked that he promise to communicate with me clearly, so we could have a clearer path forward. We agreed to resume dating. We would take turns crossing the country to see each other.

We both took Amtrak to make our weekend visits, where I would put Simba in a pet carrier. I didn't mind the thought of living in NYC and I told Joe that I'd be willing to transfer there, if his career were to keep him there longer. But he insisted he only wanted to spend one year on the East Coast. His studio was tiny, only large enough for his full-sized bed, a small desk, and the galley kitchen. With Simba and I in the place, it was packed. During my last visit to NYC, Joe asked if I trusted him. I said yes, of course. He told me to get dressed and to follow him. We ended up at Cartier on Fifth Avenue.

Joe said he couldn't have me leave the city without a symbol of our love. He bought us matching gold bands as a symbol to the world we were committed to one another and the future was ours, together. I was in shock, but I absolutely loved it.

On the Amtrak back to DC, I ran into my close friend Tony, who was also returning from a weekend in NYC. Tony knew everything about me and all of my boy drama, so I was apprehensive about telling him how my weekend with Joe had gone. Tony was always candid about the guys I dated and situations I found myself in, I appreciated him for that. The shiny new ring on my left hand stood out since I was sitting next to the window on the train, with

Tony to my left. There was no hiding it. Once his jaw was off of the floor, Tony asked me what had happened that weekend. I filled him in on the chain of events with Joe, his move, and my willingness to maintain a long-distance relationship. Tony listened to all my romantic rationalizations about why this was all okay, and he cautiously supported me.

On Joe's final weekend visit to DC, my friends David and Keith hosted a holiday white party in DC. This event would serve as Joe's coronation into my larger circle of friends. My ex-husband Sampson would also be in attendance. This would be the first time we had seen each other in a year. Sampson and I's friend circles overlapped, as we navigated the tactful divorce waters. Joe and I wore similar outfits.

Sampson was at the opposite end of the party with his best friend Doug and another friend of theirs, who I also knew well. I nervously approached and I introduced them to Joe. I worried they would ridicule me for being in a relationship again so soon and wearing rings, but they remained cordial. After the party, Sampson sent me a message via Facebook, noting that we had only been divorced for a year, out of concern I was moving too quickly with Joe. I thanked him for his concern and assured him I was fine.

Once Joe returned to New York, we continued our frequent calls. One day, Joe told me his best female friend from LA would be moving into his small studio apartment. She had lost her job and wanted to start her life over. I pushed back, asking where I would stay the next time I visited him. Joe had no answer; he simply refused to talk anymore about it, saying it was a done deal. He added that he was too busy with work and mentally exhausted. He then asked for three weeks to think about things between us.

Even I recognized these serious red flags.

Towards the conclusion of the three-week period, I came home tipsy one night. Out of a nagging suspicion, I downloaded Grindr and zeroed in on the area where he lived. As I scrolled through the images, Joe's photo popped up. His profile listed as a single bottom and new to NYC. Hurt and confused, I looked at the gold band on my finger. How had we gone so quickly from Cartier to Grindr? I would've understood his desire to meet new guys and play in the city, but why put up this elaborate charade of wanting monogamy and family life? (We had discussed an open relationship while we lived apart, but he claimed to not want that.) I immediately made frantic calls to my relationship experts. Tony, David, and Keith listened to my sad story and agreed that it was a good idea to distance myself from Joe.

Joe and I had a FaceTime call two days later, after I reminded him it had been three weeks and that's what he had asked for. I weighed whether to tell him I'd seen his Grindr profile. Joe suddenly asked if I knew what a glory hole was. Before I could respond, he informed me that he had gone to one with a friend. This was the final nail in the coffin. Who in their right mind goes to a glory hole and then tells their lover? Besides, Joe was potentially exposing me to HIV and STIs via his Grindr explorations, since we weren't using protection. He failed to see my concerns. At the end of this call, I made the decision to end things with Joe.

I wasn't mad at Joe; I was disappointed more than anything. And perplexed at the extremes he went to, to tell me he was in it for the long haul. The future was a little scary. I would move to Fresno as planned, but as a single man. I was also ashamed that I would have to explain this development to my new employer, since they knew of Joe. Since I was now single, I would no longer require a relocation to join Joe in LA or San Francisco. I worried that I would get stuck in Fresno.

Months later, Joe and I met up in person in Modesto, California, when he was in San Francisco for a family funeral. For clarity, Joe and I talked things out face to face at an Olive Garden, which was his choice, not mine. At a minimum I would get to eat as many breadsticks as I wanted. I didn't wish or need to make him feel badly; I just wanted to understand. I explained how sad I was that he claimed to love me, but his secretive sex play told me a different story. Joe grew teary and swore he wanted a future with me. But then he admitted to dating a guy in NYC he met on Grindr. While I was processing that, he switched gears again and promised to move back to San Francisco in March, since I was "the one." Joe insisted that he needed me in his life and he wanted to have a family with me.

I could not understand his mixed signals, even now, but I still cared for him. Except the road to romance between us was already riddled with many potholes. Joe tearfully asked for another chance. Since I was solo and not seeing anyone, I hesitantly agreed. But in my heart, I knew it wouldn't work. Joe started sharing his location with me on his iPhone, to help rebuild trust. We communicated for about two weeks. I started to notice that his locations didn't always align with what he was telling me. Finally, I found out that Joe was still seeing someone. For the umpteenth time, I was officially done with him.

Writing all of this about Joe now, I know, makes me look and feel like a complete moron. But as I relive the relationship, at least I'm certain the failure with Joe wasn't my fault. Lord knows I tried. The Cartier ring sits in its box in my safe. I haven't seen Joe since and I will give it back to him if our paths ever cross again.

I had one final trip to take with the Secret Service at the end of February 2019 and it was a grand one. I jumped on a trip to LA, so I could make a trip up to Fresno to meet my new officemates and do a day's worth of apartment hunting. The night before, I would be going to the Grammy Awards. This would be my last hurrah—and it was fitting that it would be one involving music. My country singer aspirations had fallen to the back burner, in light of the significant life changes under way but attending these award shows were always a dream of mine. I donned my best suit and headed to the Staples Center early, gaining access due to my credentials. The protectee, Michelle Obama, would be part of the show opening, after Camila Cabello performed the song "Havana."

While waiting backstage, I saw giants like Dolly Parton, Ricky Martin, BTS—and even Lady Gaga. This was a place that I'd always hoped to be one day, as a singer-performer. I had dreamed as a child of walking out on stage to accept an award, give an acceptance speech, and hear the music fading me out as they cut to a commercial. I was immersed in that world – but in a much different role than I had ever imagined.

I pondered if I could have ever made it as a star if I had set my mind to it. Was it too much to ask, to have one album and hear one song on the radio? All of these thoughts were racing through my mind as I stood among music royalty. I saw Alicia Keys, Lady Gaga, Jada Pinkett Smith, and J. Lo walk to the stage to immense applause. As Michelle Obama began to speak, the Staples Center erupted in cheers and applause, longer than for any stars.

It was goose-bump moments like these that I would miss the most about my Secret Service job. I never took this job for granted, despite occasional complaining. I was humbled by the role I played, protecting the most important people in the world, and I never lost sight of that. Despite my show business aspirations, I was never in the spotlight. Nobody was ever looking at me. I had learned to live with that. I was behind the scenes, but I had a huge responsibility.

Back in DC, in March 2019, my management company found a tenant for my condo that aligned with my departure date. It came time to pack up. I started in my office. That was a poor place to start, given the feels I began to encounter as I was pulling stuff off of the bookshelf. The first were personally signed books by Barack and Michelle Obama. I had grown to admire, appreciate, and be in awe of these amazing people. I had spent over two years traveling the world with them, flying on G5s, meeting globally influential people, and visiting places people only dream about. All of that came flooding back to me as I packed things up.

The Secret Service had been so much of my identity over the last decade, I wasn't sure I knew how to separate myself from it. The demands and stresses of an agent are so unique, there's no way I would ever find that experience in another job. But I had to take the chance. I don't live with regrets and I did not want to end life with the regret of not having a child. I would be remiss if I didn't admit I was scared and a little frightened as I packed up my life into boxes, not knowing what life would look like when I unpacked them in California. Starting over is hard; it's even harder when you don't know anything about the place you're going, or don't know anyone in your new surroundings. My professional life would soon be completely new.

It took two weeks for me to pack up everything and sell the items I wouldn't be taking to Fresno. I gave a few things to Sampson from our former home. We saw each other only socially, at happy hours with our overlapping group of friends, but were on good terms. I had even met some of the guys he had dated. We were in a good place and I was happy for it.

The movers arrived on March 22nd and loaded up their truck, leaving in my condo only an air mattress, a few suitcases, Simba, and myself. My stuff wouldn't arrive in Fresno for a couple of weeks, so I had time to tie up loose ends in DC and then begin the westward trek. As had become my compulsion, I rewarded my big life change by making a visit to the Audi dealer. I had seen a 2018 Audi S4 Prestige online, completely decked out, and thought it would make a great car to drive across the country. Completely and utterly ridiculous, I know, but I bought it anyway. I'm certain I channel some kind of psychiatric disorder through my car purchases.

On my last night in my condo, my close and platonic friend David came to spend the evening with me. David is good at knowing when his support may be needed without even asking and this was one of those occasions. He played with Simba in my empty condo and then we went for dinner and drinks at Freddie's Beach Bar in Crystal City. Freddie's was always a good time for singing karaoke, drag shows, or a decent meal in a fun environment. Freddie has been a pillar of the gay community for decades and it was fitting for us to spend my last evening in Arlington there.

The next day was my last day at work. It was completely anti-climactic. There was one boss in the office, a man who was always nonchalant and didn't even leave his office. I turned in my gear to our administrative assistant., Then I oddly sat around for a few minutes, before I realized there was no point in it. After all, I no longer had an issued cell phone, laptop, or gun. That meant I no longer had any identity or purpose there.

There was no goodbye lunch, due to the inability to plan things in the fluid realm of protection, no farewell address, no good-luck card, no exit interview, no nothing. Almost a decade of dedicated service had suddenly come to an end. It was fitting for the agency to not mark my departure, as I was never as special as I had thought. While I may have worked harder than some, I was always a cog in the wheel, and the machine rolls on without missing a beat. None of it surprised me. I had witnessed it countless times before, when competent agents walked away from the agency. Nobody stopped them to ask why or what could be done to keep them with the agency. It projected the mentality of "good riddance" to the departing agents since there was always going to be a line of new agents wanting to work there. The company policy was that we were lucky to work there.

I was in good company when it comes to leaving; I was the seventeenth Special Agent from my graduating class of twenty-three to walk away in search of a greener pasture. None of my classmates of mine had returned to the Service, which says a lot.

My last few nights in DC were fun—but sloppy. I was staying at Doug's place since we had remained friends through the Sampson breakup and I had known him just as long. One night I went to the gay bar Number 9 for happy hour with a colleague. Later, more friends showed up. I don't recall the walk home, but video exists of me laying on Doug's floor around 11:00 PM, three sheets to the wind, and asking about my dog. Saturday night was my final night in town, before I was to head to Richmond to see my family. It was a casual evening with lots of friends showing up for dinner at Commissary in Logan Circle to see me off. There was a group of six really close friends who knew everything about me. They had been there for me from the month I arrived in DC, through my divorce, through all of my bitching and moaning about my career, and through all of the boyfriend drama I forced upon them. These were the guys I chose as my family. After dinner, we went for drinks at Number 9 and then the gay dive bar Trade. There was an ongoing flow of friends and acquaintances who would show up for a drink or two and then leave, but the closest friends stayed with me throughout. As the night went on, we all ended up at Pitchers in Adams Morgan. As we hugged tightly, I became "that guy" crying in a bar.

It was time to share painful goodbyes. I loved David and Keith and would miss having them close by as my pillars. They'd been there for me from the month I moved to DC and were by my side during all of the life changes I'd endured. Tony was my wingman and a really good one, too. He was supportive in all the right ways, protecting me as needed, and I had confided things I had never told anyone. I had sought his advice countless times regarding boys, and we had often traveled together. We knew we would continue our relationship, but it would change, as all things do. I had grown to love him. After more goodbyes and more waterworks, we all left the bar and went our separate ways, emotionally exhausted from the night.

The next morning, I loaded up the car and Simba and I made

the short drive to Richmond to spend the night with Mom, then visit my sister, her family, and pop over to see my brother. It had become routine to visit Mom once a month, so this didn't feel any different. Mom said she was excited to visit California and I appreciated her outlook on my move. She had never traveled any farther west than Missouri and now she had a reason to. Mom had grown accustomed to her youngest son living away from home and she didn't appear to treat this move any differently.

Early the next day, I loaded up the car, asked Mom to take a photo before I began my cross-country drive, and we said our goodbyes. Mom still lives in the town where I grew up, so I was leaving a very familiar place. Before Simba and I reached the Interstate, I stopped at a 7/11 for coffee. That's when I saw the owner of the restaurant where I had my first job. I hadn't seen him in years. I filled him in on my new life. I'm convinced I wouldn't be where I am today without Scott gambling on a fifteen-year-old me; I learned so much working for him. It was fitting that he was the last person I'd see before leaving it all behind. The world's a funny place.

I broke the drive up into five days. I stopped along the way a lot due to needing to walk Simba, who was patiently sitting in the shotgun seat. He was bored out of his mind, stuck in a car for five days, but he handled it well. We stopped to see random things like the Cadillac Ranch in Amarillo, Texas, and enjoyed the beautiful drive from northern Arizona down to Phoenix. I was in awe at the beauty of that route and the Audi wanted to run between 80-100mph. The car drove like it was on rails and I was always eager to put more power to the Quattro system. I'm surprised I didn't get stopped for speeding, but the roads were mostly wide open on the drive. I sang country songs until I couldn't sing anymore, thought about everything and anything, talked to Simba, made phone calls, played with every option I could find on the car, listed to a Spanish radio station for an entire day, and did anything else to occupy my mind.

It wasn't until I was halfway across Texas that I accidentally hit a button and activated the car's lane assist function. This, combined with the adaptive cruise control, made the car semi-autonomous. It would drive itself for a period of time before reminding me to use the steering wheel. I used the system a lot and it worked really well. We stayed a night in LA with a guy I had met in Vegas during Matinee, with who I had the best toe-curling give me that D sex I had experienced in my life, as a top and a bottom. The next day Simba and I started the final leg of the trip: the three-hour drive to Fresno.

We arrived at our new home safely, pulling up to the brand-new gated apartment community, a week before the movers would arrive, especially because I had to accept a sofa delivery the next morning. The buildings were only two stories high and I chose a second-story unit with unobstructed views of the Sierra Nevada mountains. The rent was inexpensive compared to anywhere else I'd lived recently. I wouldn't begin work for another week yet.

Life in Fresno was fine. I returned to using gay apps to try and meet people. I was twenty minutes from the small gay part of town, the Tower district, and close to Fresno State campus. Work was far more mundane than the high tempo high thrill world I had just left, but it felt great to have set hours, no constant travel-ing, and weekends off. Oddly, my first day on the job was exactly one year after I had my meltdown in Mexico, where I found the resolve to find a new path forward. Fresno wasn't thrilling, exciting, or enthralling, but it was fine. I felt isolated there, three hours from LA and three hours from San Francisco, but it provided time and space to calm my mind and allow myself a chance to breathe, for the first time in years. If you have a family and love the heat, it's a good spot to be. Cost of living is low and Clovis has great school districts. But it's the central valley of CA. There is nothing but fields and tumbleweeds along I-99. Fresno weather was awful for Simba, who has two coats. This meant not walking him until the sun went down and temperatures dropped below 100.

The gay scene was small but friendly. I was initially wary of socializing, since I didn't plan on living there very long, but I needed the socialization. Based on what I'd seen on the apps, the local options were college guys with daddy issues or couples who were in open relationships. I was flattered to be pursued by attractive younger men, but I quickly realized we had nothing in common and on one occasion during oral sex, a guy told me he had just gotten his own cell phone plan. That ended the fun with younger men. There were a few gays bars, FAB and Legends being the most popular. On my first visit to FAB on a Sunday afternoon, an older guy named James saw I was new and introduced himself. I met his group of friends, including one guy who worked for Kamala Harris, since we would be able to discuss politics.

I ended up spending most of my time socializing with James and his friendly group. Legends bar was good for dancing on Saturday nights but charged a $20 cover, way too high for Fresno. I was impressed with how accepting the Fresno community was. During Pride weekend, there was a healthy mix of heterosexuals among the LGBTQ celebrants. Not bad for a Republican area.

Work in Fresno was okay, crazy busy the first two months, during which I received half a dozen complaints or new cases on a single day. I was receiving a baptism by fire and needed to adapt quickly, to keep up with the workload and learn the new systems. I was working with a former Secret Service agent from the Washington Field Office. He had left the agency three years prior to me and was happy in his new life out west, but he wasn't thrilled with Fresno and hoped to transfer soon.

As I sat in Fresno, I began reflecting on my life and one thing stood out as unresolved. Hollywood, mom's abusive ex-boyfriend. I never had closure regarding that chapter in my life, though my siblings had resolved their feelings long ago, it took me a lot longer. Feeling the time was right, I located Hollywood on Facebook and sent him the following message.

"Good morning. I hope this finds you well. I cannot explain why, but after almost 20 years, something told me to contact you. The years have flown by, life has changed us all, & as we continue to age, it's important to acknowledge and properly put to bed things from the past. You had a profound effect on me during my early life. You were a father figure when I didn't exactly have one and for that, thank you. The bad times had a lasting effect on me for many years after but as time tends to do, it heals. I honestly think that due to the early interactions with law enforcement, it led me into that career field again, I can thank you for that as I love what I do. I hope you and your family are well, happy, and wish you nothing but the best."

Though I don't think he ever read it and never responded, that's okay; it was closure enough for me.

From the time I arrived in Fresno, I never allowed myself to envision a future there. I was longing to finally put down roots, but Fresno was not where I wanted that to occur. It was always seen as a brief layover location until I transferred to a larger city with better pay and dating options. My officemates were not aware that Joe and I were no longer together; I was worried that being single would get me stuck in Fresno. Joe had been my ticket to LA or San Francisco.

During the two weeks where Joe and I had quasi-reconciled, a position came available in the San Francisco office. I requested a transfer, since it was a far better location, with or without Joe. San Francisco would also set me up for a higher pension in retirement. In August 2019, I was granted the transfer. It was refreshing to work for an agency that cares for its people and follows through on what they say. My case was extremely rare, transferring offices after only six months, but it worked in the best interest of everyone and didn't cost the agency a dime. Nor did the division lose an agent.

I leased a studio apartment and formally moved to San Francisco in October 2019. And here is where I began my memoir.

Life in San Francisco has been great so far, notwithstanding the high rent. You can't beat the walkability of the city and all it has to offer, except for when COVID-19 closes most establishments, as it did in March 2020. Even still, the pandemic downtime allowed me, for the first time in a decade, to assess my life and to allow my mind to catch up with my body.

From early on in my life, I hid who I really was due to uncertainty, repressive environmental and social factors, and mostly homophobia. I denied myself the ability to be happy, out of fear of what other people would think and how it would affect my career. This is not unique to me; these are things millions of people face every day. Though I was delayed in coming out, I had most of my family supporting me along the way. Many people aren't as fortunate and I'm thankful for my good fortunes. When it came to my career, I plotted my way forward while displaying a masculine exterior that I thought worked best to achieve my goals. This led to some self-loathing, but with time and maturity it subsided. The world of law enforcement is still a straight male-dominated world but as time passes and the cries for equality get louder, I'm optimistic it'll also change.

It's been a wild and crazy ride, one I never imagined I would be on. As I reflect at where I have been, it seems surreal. I often wonder where I got my "traveling bones" and can't help but think it stemmed from living in numerous varying homes growing up and the miles and lots of traveling to visit relatives. Intermix that with the influence of music from an early age, and teen desires to be a country singer-performer. That never happened, but as a Secret Service agent I was able to travel the world and visit places very few people ever get to. I was able to stand on stages around the world in front of thousands of people and be part of that action, even if in the periphery during Michelle Obama's book tour. I was able to see how the wealthy and powerful live their lives. My journey crossed paths with successful musicians and I could observe the world I never entered. The path I led certainly allowed me to have the soul of a sailor and never sit still, even if it was sometimes to my own detriment as a person seeking to put down roots. I wasn't able to fully relax or truly enjoy what was going on around me, since I was always focused on what's ahead. My mind was always racing and planning, and I could not turn it off. I felt I had to work harder and longer to prove myself, ensuring I was as indispensable as possible in the event my sexuality interfered with my career. Because of all of it, I missed a lot of my life—and often times didn't know it until it was too late.

It took over a year after leaving the Service to mentally decompress and calm my mind. Sheltering in place during the COVID pandemic helped achieve that self-examination. I finally recognized I was trying to create this ideal life, when the one in front of me was already spectacular. After moving to California, I kept a plan in my mind to eventually move back east but I finally realized that would have perpetuated the same cycle, one I had to break free from. Frequent moves provide a change of scene, but seriously prevented me from establishing myself and putting down the roots that are necessary to build a relationship and have a family. With every move, it set me back even farther, as I continued to age. I can't and won't do that any longer. This is my home, this is where I'll make it happen.

I don't have regrets for my past; that's not how I operate. Every man who has been in my life has played an important role or taught me an important lesson I needed to learn. I don't hold grudges or ill feelings toward any of them; life is too short for that.

Sampson taught me more than I can ever write in a book. I wouldn't be who I am or where I am without him and I'm forever thankful he was in my life and that we have been able to remain friends since our divorce. Alex, the catalyst that ended things with Sampson, saved me from myself. Alex ignited a fire inside of me I hadn't known before and was the awakening I needed before things got even worse. Alex and I haven't talked in two years and that's okay. Ben taught me selflessness in a relationship, and Colin taught me what not to do in a relationship. That is, allowing work to dictate your personal life and coldly hurting someone who cares about you. Joe taught me that relationships aren't built on designer clothes and five-star hotel getaways; they are built on trust and honesty. I was able to let down my walls with Joe, to be my true self without fear of judgement. Without him, it's likely I would have turned down the Fresno job and certainly not gotten a transfer to San Francisco, I'm very thankful for that.

The music in my life has served as a companion, a connective tissue, a constant security blanket. Certain tunes bring back a flood of memories that were established in the points of time that are forever tied to them. I cannot undo these visceral and sometimes raw memories, nor would I want to. They serve as important reminders of where I have been and how I have gotten here. A song may take me back to a different time and place, but I allow myself only a brief visit to the past. I'm all about the present and future now.

All of these people, experiences, and songs filled unique roles in my life, shining light where needed, to ensure I present my true self to the world. These forces now allow me to treat Johnny, my new boyfriend, with the respect, compassion, love, understanding, and maturity he deserves. No longer do I sacrifice myself to a romance; I have learned to look out for my own interests as well. I had to break free from the cruel societal norms cast upon me. I had to break free from the cycle of running, the fear of putting down roots. I had to break free from the traps in life, both in my control and out of my control. I had to break free from the rat race to see the great things already in front of me, in the here and now.

Printed in the USA
CPSIA information can be obtained
at www.ICGtesting.com
LVHW011302051223
765657LV00002B/39